PRODUCT DESIGN

latex
clothes

This book is for Peter, Evelyn, Siobhan and Grainne

making
latex
clothes

sian-kate mooney

BT Batsford

First Published 2004

Text and diagrams/drawings © Sian-Kate Mooney 2004

The right of Sian-Kate Mooney to be identified as Author of this work has been asserted by him in accordance with the Copyright, Designs and Patents Act 1988.

ISBN 0 7134 8865 4

A CIP catalogue record for this book is available from the British Library.

Volume © B T Batsford

Printed in Malaysia

for the publishers

B T Batsford
Chrysalis Books Group
The Chrysalis Building
Bramley Road
London W10 6SP

www.batsford.com

An imprint of **Chrysalis** Books Group

Front cover: Photograph by Sarah Dewe. Model Martina Donahower.

Contents

Foreword

What is latex rubber? Natural rubber, India rubber or caoutchouc are all names for the solid and elastic material made from the 'milk' or latex of various plants. These may be found all over the world. The most common natural source of latex in the UK, for example, is the dandelion. If you snap a dandelion stalk, it will emit white fluid latex that will dry to produce rubber. Commercially, however, latex is harvested from *Hevea braziliensi*, or the latex-producing tree, which grows in the world's tropical forests.

Latex is obtained commercially by wounding the tree: a sloping incision is cut in the bark and the milk-like substance that 'bleeds' out is collected regularly over several years. This does not harm the tree which, when past its useful life producing latex, is used as timber. Like other natural, as opposed to man-made, materials, latex rubber slowly and completely degrades, so that when latex products are finally disposed of they do not harm the environment.

Christopher Columbus introduced latex to Europe in 1496 when he sailed back from the West Indies with the first rubber balls. Previous balls had been made of stuffed leather – there was no comparison as these balls actually bounced! The Spaniards became the first to use latex in Europe, when they discovered its ability to waterproof fabrics. Later, in 1818, Charles Macintosh re-discovered and perfected the technique, hence the 'Macintosh'.

Over the centuries latex has been subject to many chemicals and processes, such as mastication and vulcanization, so that a whole range of applications could be developed. Latex as we know it today is used for a thousand different and diverse products, ranging from hot-water bottles to surgeons' gloves and car tyres.

It was in the 1950s that latex was probably first associated with high fashion, when it became linked with Rock and Roll music and the Teddy Boys, who wore latex crêpe soles on the bottom of their blue suede shoes.

In the 1960s, latex garments were advertised in the backs of newspapers and magazines. These were made from 'dipped' shapes to form very basic pants and T-shirts. They were euphemistically sold as 'slimming' aids and it was contended that wearing these garments would help you lose weight. One could have indeed done this, but the only weight lost would have been through excessive perspiration! With hindsight I think it would be fair to say that most people subscribing to these crude items of clothing were early latex fetishists fulfilling their desire to wear rubber next to their skin.

The method of making latex clothes by dipping is still used, as it is a cost-effective way to mass-produce simple garments. Dipping and pouring latex can produce some stunning effects and it is great fun to experiment with this technique. The only problem is that it produces a very two-dimensional garment with a poor fit. I feel that this method is therefore more suitable to jewellery and accessories.

The world of latex has a fascination for designers from clothing, film, photographic and furniture industries and this stretches to the world of avant-garde art and fetishism. The late Leigh Bowery often frequented clubs with his large frame distorted by the addition of grotesque prosthetic shapes and encased from head to toe in a shiny black latex cat-suit. At the time it was quite a disturbing and unusual sight to behold. In the last decade, however, countless clubs, societies and publications dedicated to followers of rubber fetishism have sprung up, so much so that it has become almost mainstream.

When film costume designers, such as the designers of *Batman* or *Matrix Reloaded*, chose to dress their stars in latex, it was evident that latex clothing could be used to make a strong impact. It does so not only because of its high gloss and stretch qualities, which make it extraordinarily photogenic, but also because it is seen as subversive and sexually perverted.

Fashion designers, who are known for their love of high drama, often design latex pieces for their collections. Thierry Mugler commissioned a technician to make him sheets of glitter-encrusted latex in blue and silver to create a breathtaking evening gown. Vivienne Westwood has most notably used semi-transparent nude-coloured latex for a beautifully layered and draped couture dress that gave a scintillating and subtle hint of the body moving beneath it.

Latex clothes are not easy to wear: they are cold to put on, they do not breathe, and the slightest movement causes a profusion of perspiration. Added to which, if you stand in a breeze or draught the perspiration turns icy cold. In spite of these drawbacks, many people are quite prepared to endure the discomforts in order to achieve a unique and unforgettable image.

I first became interested in making latex clothes when my fashion company was asked to design a range for Frederick's Of Hollywood, one of America's biggest mail-order catalogues. I discovered that there was little or no written technical information on how to construct latex clothes, and the people who did know jealously guarded the secret. This made me determined to master the fabrication of latex clothes, using the time-honoured method of trial and error. And the result? An order that quadrupled our turnover and won the company the Small Business Export Award 1997.

In this book, it is my intention to teach the reader the methods involved in making latex clothes. It starts with simple and basic skills, such as seam making, and gradually builds to more complicated skills, such as producing a panel dress and a boned corset. There are many different ideas for embellishing and decorating the garments as well as practical instructions on how to insert a zip (zipper) or create a press-stud opening; these ideas can be combined to produce truly unique and wearable pieces of costume or clothing.

Basic Techniques

Chapter One
Materials and equipment

Latex sheeting

This material is available in a wide variety of thicknesses, colours, and degrees of translucency. One supplier alone produces 30 colours in thicknesses ranging from 0.18mm to 1.17mm. With such a wide choice, it is possible to make an enormously varied range of garments, from sturdy belts and corsets to frilly or draped dresses.

Latex sheeting should be stored between 38 and 65 degrees centigrade away from either heaters or frost. It should also be protected from prolonged exposure to direct sunlight and artificial light with a high UV content. It is therefore best to keep latex sheeting well wrapped when in storage.

Glue

There are two types of adhesive that can be used to glue latex together – solvent and water-based. In my opinion, the solvent-based adhesives create a better bond and the seams are resistant to water.

Thinner

In order to prepare the surface of the latex to be glued, it needs to be cleaned of any excess powder that may remain from the manufacturing process. When using a solvent-based adhesive this can be done with solvent or thinner. Thinner can also be used to remove any excess glue that may have strayed beyond the garment's seams.

Trims

The most common trims used on latex clothes are zips (zippers), press studs, eyelets, buckles, rivets and boning. It must be stressed that wherever possible non-metal trims should be used, as latex becomes permanently stained brown on contact with copper, brass or bronze. Light colours may even show staining if one has recently touched coins and then the latex. When using press studs or eyelets, it is necessary to sandwich cotton tape or a woven fabric between two layers of latex to form a non-stretch anchor. Without this, the opening of the garment will stretch and the metalwork will drop out.

Boning is usually bought from a roll and easily cut with a pair of scissors. It is essential to finish the ends of boning by cutting a rounded shape and filing this smooth with some fine glasspaper. If there are any sharp ends, they may easily poke a hole through the garment and cause it to rip.

Polish

To bring the surface of the garment to a super-glossy shine, a silicone-based polish should be used. The best of these is called Micro PVC/Latex dressing. If this is not available, a silicone spray of the type found in sewing-machine shops will do the job just as well.

Talcum powder/French chalk

Either of these products may be used to dust the inside of the finished garment, ensuring that any extraneous glue does not stick the insides together. Talcum powder is the cheapest and more readily available.

Work surfaces

The gluing process can be very lengthy, as each piece has to dry thoroughly before it can be moved or assembled. To cut down on delays, I have found it highly advantageous to glue pieces on a surface that can removed from the table and set aside while the assembled pieces dry, freeing space on which to continue with the next section. Originally, I began gluing the cut pieces of latex on pattern-cutting paper known as 'spot and cross'. This has a slightly shiny surface, which enables you to peel the glued pieces away easily, and provided you rub any excess adhesive from the paper, it can be re-used over again. I now find, however, that sheets of plastic pattern card offer an even better solution, as the glued pieces can be moved away to dry with the minimum of disturbance.

Whichever surface is chosen, it is necessary to keep the area scrupulously clear of dust, grease and bits of dried glue, as the first two will stop the seams from bonding and the last will make the seams lumpy and untidy.

Receptacles

You will need at least two square or rectangular plastic pots with airtight lids measuring approximately 10cm (4in) square. These need to be free of dust and grease. The adhesive will dry quickly in the open air so it is important to pour a small amount into a pot and seal it every time you load your gluing tool. The shape of the pot simply means that there is as little wastage of the glue as possible and that the tool can be loaded evenly.

As the glue in the pot gets 'older' it will start to set into a lump. If you pour fresh glue on top it will only make the new glue unworkable, so for expediency it is better to use a clean receptacle. If you wait for the old glue to dry before cleaning a pot, it will all come out in one lump, leaving the pot ready to be filled again.

Thinner should be decanted into a glass jar with a screw-top lid or a bottle with a cork or lid to prevent it from evaporating.

Applicators

By far the best tool for applying glue is an old credit card or a similar piece of thick plastic card. Cards can be cut down to produce different sizes of spatula for gluing particular parts of the garment. If you are using a credit card, always clip off the curved edges with a sharp pair of scissors, as these will hinder the even gluing of a seam.

Rollers

A small roller is used to press the seam to ensure a strong bond. It needs to be approximately 4cm (1½in) wide and can be made from wood or plastic. A roller of the type manufactured to seal the edges of wallpaper is a perfect tool for the job.

Brushes

A large, soft, powder brush is used to dust the inside of the finished garment with talcum powder or French chalk.

Syringes

The fine, sharp hypodermic needle in a syringe is useful for extracting the air bubbles that sometimes get trapped within seams and hems. The hole left by the needle is too small to cause a weak spot in the garment (if the hole were any larger it might result in the garment tearing later).

Scalpels

Some parts of the construction processes require small holes to be slit in the latex. A very sharp craft knife or a scalpel can be used for this.

Templates

For repeated appliqué designs it is possible to create a template for the shape to be glued. The desired design can be cut with a craft knife or a scalpel from thick card or plastic pattern card. The latter will last longer and will not fray or disintegrate.

Abbreviations

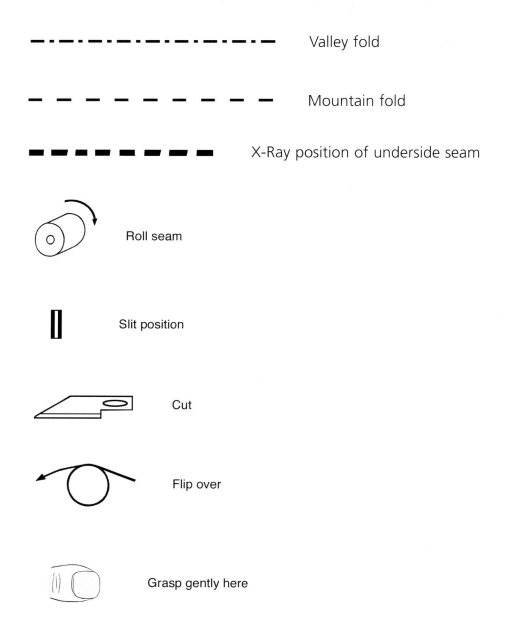

·—·—·—·—·—·—·— Valley fold

— — — — — — — — Mountain fold

■ ■ ■ ■ ■ ■ ■ X-Ray position of underside seam

Roll seam

Slit position

Cut

Flip over

Grasp gently here

R.S.U.	Right side up (shiny side of the latex facing up)
W.S.U.	Wrong side up (matt side of the latex facing up)
C.F.	Centre front of garment
C.B.	Centre back of garment
S.S.	Side seam
S.H.N.	Sleeve-head notch
F.N.	Front notch

Right side

Wrong Side

Glued Side

Chapter 2
Preparation and gluing

Essential tips

In general, making latex garments can be a tricky skill to master, as you need to be both dextrous and patient. Latex clothes-making skills are quite different from those required for any other fabric, as each panel has to be glued separately in a special sequence, this being dictated by the pattern pieces and fact that the seams are overlapped. I have already worked out the sequence of seam gluing for each garment in this book. You will find, however, that it becomes second nature after a while to know which seam needs to be glued on which side. Below are some tips on how to avoid the most common pitfalls.

- When cutting out a garment, it is helpful to remember to cut in one continuous line. If you cut an uneven line with fine tags, these can very easily become the first part of a tear. The uneven tags will not weaken the garment once it is made (although they look messy); it is when you try to pull the seam apart to reposition it that the latex is more than likely to tear. Some people use a rotary cutter to ensure that the cut edges are smooth and free of tags.

- I recommend that you only clean with thinner the area that is to be glued. A sheet of latex that has had every scrap of talcum powder removed becomes very sticky and static and is almost impossible to work with.

- Always make sure that the seams to be glued are scrupulously cleaned of talcum powder, dust and grease. Unless this has been done, the seam allowances will never stick together.

- Glue dries faster in a warm room. This can have advantages, but it is sometimes preferable to work in a cooler room. If you are gluing around intricate curves, for example, and covering small areas of seam allowance slowly, it is better that the glue stays viscose for as long as possible to allow for repositioning.

- Once the separate garment sections have been glued, you can leave them lying flat for about a day before you assemble the pieces. Any longer and the glue gets covered in a small layer of dust and goes off. The seams may appear to stick together at the time, but the garment may fall apart later.

- Keep the powdering and polishing areas separate and confined. During the manufacturing process, it is easy for these two products to stray onto glued seams and trims, rendering them non-sticky.

Health and safety

When working with latex sheeting, it is important to follow health and safety guidelines.

- Solvent-based adhesives are highly flammable and should only be used in a well-ventilated area.

- The adhesive is a solution of a compound of natural latex dissolved in petroleum solvents, usually methanol or ethanol. For this reason, it is essential to use gloves or a good barrier cream and avoid contact as much as possible with the glue or thinner.

- Latex sheeting is flammable and should be protected from naked flames during handling and storing.

- Latex may cause an allergic reaction and should be avoided if this occurs.

- It is advisable to observe no-smoking restrictions when using all the above products.

Making notches

As with any garment, notches are an essential code for identifying specific parts of the pattern piece and as a guide to even seam matching. I have found that cut notches not only look ugly, but also create a weak point that is liable to rip when the garment is under construction. Instead of cutting notches, I use a water-based felt-tip marker to indicate the notch on the wrong side of the latex.

A simple dot is enough to denote where the notch lies. If you are using pale-coloured latex do not use a strong colour, such as red or black, as this will leave a stain. I find light grey a good choice. With a black or the darker-coloured latex, you do not have to be so careful and a biro mark will suffice. Both felt-tip pen and biro can be removed later with thinner.

A simple seam

The following samples are worth making up, as they are designed to cover all the basic skills you will need to make most simple latex clothes and all the examples in this book. Straight seams are used in virtually all garments and offer a good way of learning the basic principles of cleaning, gluing and joining a seam.

Unlike sewn seams, glued seams are overlapped, ideally by 8mm ($^5/_{16}$in). Different seam allowances are used to produce specific effects. Unless I give an alternative measurement, it should be taken that 8mm ($^5/_{16}$in) is the standard seam allowance.

1

```
SIMPLE SEAM
PIECE A
R.S.U.
CLEANING
```

```
SIMPLE SEAM
PIECE B
W.S.U.
CLEANING
```

1 Cut two pieces of latex sheeting approximately 7 x 4cm (3 x 1½in). Place the two pieces of latex you are about to join in front of you. With the right (shiny) side of piece A facing up (R.S.U.), clean the seam allowance to be glued with thinner. Set it aside and leave it to dry. With the wrong (rough) side of piece B facing up (W.S.U.), clean the seam allowance to be glued with thinner. Set it aside and leave it to dry.

2

```
SIMPLE SEAM
PIECE A
R.S.U.
GLUING
```

```
SIMPLE SEAM
PIECE B
W.S.U.
GLUING
```

2 Pour enough glue into a pot to cover the bottom. Take a broad-edged spatula (about the width of a standard credit card with the curved edges cut off) and dip it into the glue. Cover the pot and turn to your sample. Place the spatula on piece A, 8mm (5/16in) away from the cleaned edge, holding it at an angle of about 45 degrees. Draw it towards you, lifting it away from the work surface as soon as the seam has been covered with glue. Repeat this process on piece B.

3

```
SIMPLE SEAM
PIECE B
R.S.U.

SIMPLE SEAM
PIECE A
R.S.U.
JOINING
```

3 Turn over piece B, with the right side facing up, and gently place it on piece A to overlap the two glued strips. At this stage you can check that the pieces are positioned exactly where you want. If they are not, they have not yet bonded and can easily be pulled apart and repositioned. When you are satisfied that the two seam allowances are correctly joined, take the roller and roll along the length of the seam. It is now secure but will take 24 hours to become permanently bonded.

Curved seam

The curved seam and the straight seam are the joins that are most commonly used when constructing any latex garment. The curved seam is a little tricky to master at first, but with practice it will become second nature.

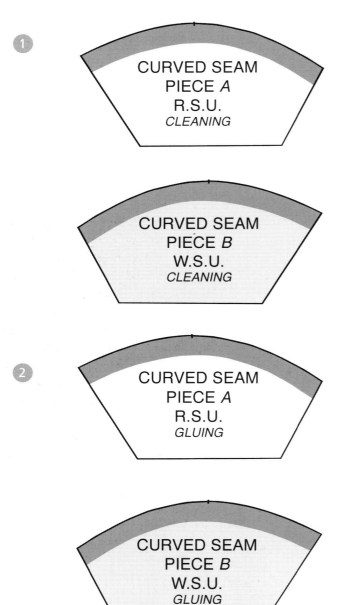

1 Cut and assemble two identical curved pieces, as shown in the diagrams. Mark the notch position. With the right side of piece A facing up (R.S.U.), clean the seam allowance. Repeat for piece B with W.S.U. Set both pieces aside to dry.

2 Cut a spatula around 4cm (1½in) wide and start to glue 8mm (⁵⁄₁₆in) away from the edge. If you use a few strokes with a narrower breadth, taking the spatula from the inner edge of the seam allowance to the outer edge, it is possible to achieve a curve in a series of straight edges. This is a better method than cutting a spatula the width of the seam allowance and following around the curve, as the spatula tends to 'scuff' against the edge and create an uneven, lumpy, seam. Glue along the seam allowance of piece A and then piece B and allow both to dry.

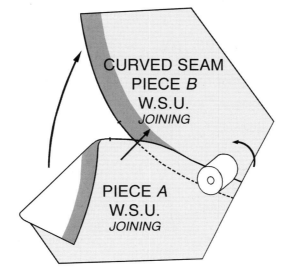

3   Turn over piece A and join the beginning of the seam together.

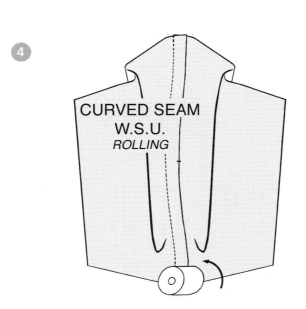

4   Gently press this point and gradually work your way along the seam, taking care to keep the seam allowance even. If you have to stretch piece B slightly to get around the curve, make sure that the underside, piece A, is also stretched to compensate. It will now become apparent why a notch is needed. As you come to the notch you can gauge if you have stretched one piece more than the other. Should this be the case you can gently pull the pieces apart and re-do the seam. Once you are happy with the seam, firmly roll along the length of it to secure the bond.

Simple hem

Hemming has two main functions: it gives the garment a quality finish, and it seals the end of each seam, strengthening it at its weakest point. Some garments do not have hems, but these happen to be the more inexpensive dipped latex pieces, which have no seams.

Generally a hem is a 1cm ($^3/_8$in) turning unless it is on a sharp curve. Here the same rule applies to latex as for any fabric: for a neat finish, the sharper the curve the smaller the seam allowance. The smallest turning I have used is 0.5cm ($^1/_4$in), on a pair of bikini bottoms. Conversely, you may want to use a larger turning as a design feature.

You will also notice in the garment construction diagrams that in most instances I hem the separate sections before any seams are put together, leaving about 2cm ($^3/_4$in) unhemmed next to any seam. Once the seam is put together, it is easy to complete the hem. This helps to reduce the chances of the whole piece of work balling up. It is very difficult to make a neat circular hem around a finished piece without the insides of the garment sticking together, especially if the hem in question is around a narrow cuff. Using this method you can make the greater part of the hem on the 'flat' and get a really neat finish.

1

1 Cut a piece of latex approximately 6 x 14cm (2½ x 5½in). Clean and glue a 2cm (¾in) strip along one of the long edges.

2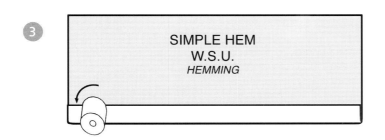

2 When dry, fold up one side of the glued piece by 1cm (⅜in). Make sure that the beginning is folded up to create a right angle. If you start the hem off at an odd angle, you will have either a dwindling or growing hem. Place the roller on the hem and apply pressure. With the other hand grasp the hem at the opposite end and gently pull against the roller. This will automatically fold the seam over. As a general rule, the more you stretch the smaller the seam allowance will be.

3

3 Adjust the stretch to give a 1cm (⅜in) turning and roll towards the opposite end to finish.

Simple dart

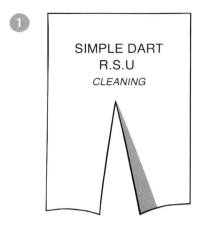

1 Cut a sample piece with an even-sided slit, as shown. With the right side facing up (R.S.U.), clean the right edge of the dart. Allow it to dry.

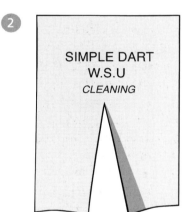

2 Turn over and with the wrong side facing up (W.S.U.) clean the right edge of the dart again.

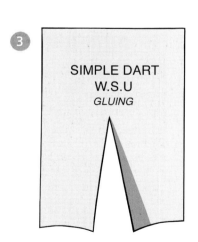

3 Follow the same sequence but this time gluing the edge of the dart on both sides. The portion glued should start 1mm ($1/24$in) above the point of the dart and should be triangular in shape, 1mm ($1/24$in) at the top and 8mm ($5/16$in) at the bottom.

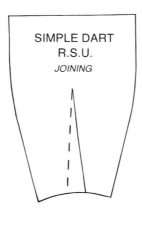

SIMPLE DART
R.S.U.
JOINING

a
b

SIMPLE DART
R.S.U.
JOINING

4 Start to form the dart at the top, overlapping the seams at an angle that eventually makes points a and b meet.

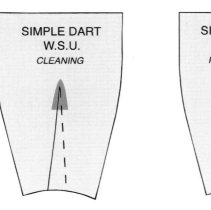

SIMPLE DART
W.S.U.
CLEANING

SIMPLE DART
W.S.U.
REINFORCING

5 If the dart is to be under a lot of tension, it may be necessary to reinforce the top where the overlap is most narrow. This can be achieved by adding a small triangle of latex. Cut, clean and glue the reinforcing triangle in the normal way, and press it onto the point of the dart, which itself has been cleaned and glued.

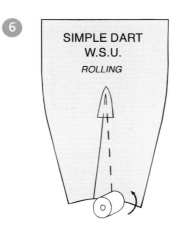

SIMPLE DART
W.S.U.
ROLLING

6 Roll firmly along the dart to bond.

Gathering

Gatherings can be used for any part of a latex garment where they would normally be found in fabric clothes. They are particularly successful when used for puff sleeves, blouson jackets, gathered skirts and bikini bra cups.

GATHER
PIECE A
R.S.U.
CLEANING

GATHER
PIECE B
R.S.U.
CLEANING

1   As with the previous seams, clean seam allowances on the right side of piece A (the frill) and the wrong side of piece B (the 'body'). Mark in the notches, dividing each seam into quarters.

GATHER
PIECE A
R.S.U.
GLUING

GATHER
PIECE B
R.S.U.
GLUING

2   Apply the glue to each seam allowance.

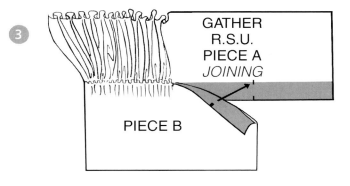

3 GATHER
R.S.U.
PIECE A
JOINING

PIECE B

3   Turn over piece B and just touch the beginning of the seams together. Start making the frill by stretching piece B over A, matching the notches as you go. You will notice that this starts to form a frill. The more you stretch piece B, the more frill will be created.

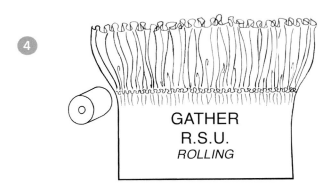

4 GATHER
R.S.U.
ROLLING

4   Roll over the glued seam again to bond the seam allowances together.

Regular pleats

Once you have worked out the gluing sequence, you will find that pleats are quite simple to construct. It is often helpful to make a paper mock-up of a pleated section in miniature, as in the diagram, so that you can keep referring to it and avoid too much confusion.

1

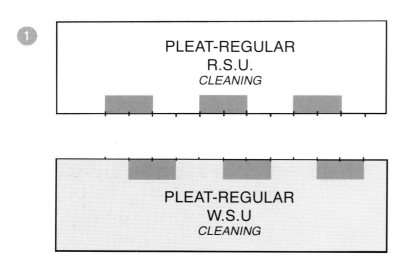

PLEAT-REGULAR
R.S.U.
CLEANING

PLEAT-REGULAR
W.S.U
CLEANING

1   Cut a piece of latex 14 x 5 (5¹/₂ x 2in). Mark the gluing sequence on the latex with a felt-tip pen. To ensure that the measurements are accurate and the pleats are of the desired uniform size, use a ruler or tape measure. Clean both sides of the piece to be pleated. On this sample, the pleat is glued to a depth and width of 1cm (³/₈in), but pleats can, of course, be glued down to any desired depth and width.

2

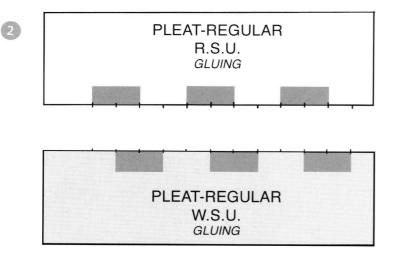

PLEAT-REGULAR
R.S.U.
GLUING

PLEAT-REGULAR
W.S.U.
GLUING

2   For this sample, use a 2cm (³/₄in) spatula to apply glue to the right side. The size of the spatula is specified here as it is the exact width of the area to be glued in this instance, which makes the process more efficient and accurate. Allow to dry thoroughly. Glue the wrong side of the piece in the sequence illustrated. Again, allow the piece to dry thoroughly.

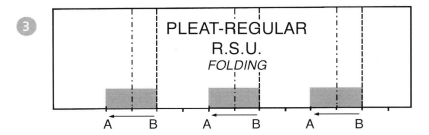

PLEAT-REGULAR
R.S.U.
FOLDING

A   B   A   B   A   B

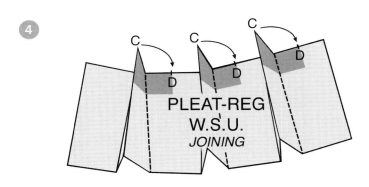

C   C   C

D   D   D

PLEAT-REG
W.S.U.
JOINING

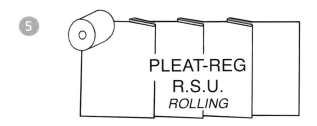

PLEAT-REG
R.S.U.
ROLLING

3 With the right side facing up, bring point B to point A. The fold between these two points is a valley fold. Make sure that the fold is at a right angle, and that the cut edge overlaps itself exactly. It is essential to be accurate in order to produce a pleat that hangs vertically. If the points do not meet each other exactly, you can gently peel them apart and re-position them.

4 Turn the work over so that the wrong side is now facing up (W.S.U.) and fold points C to D. The mountain fold in illustration 3 becomes a valley fold when turned W.S.U..

5 Lay the work flat and roll the glued parts firmly to bond them.

Box pleats

Making a box pleat is a similar process to making a regular pleat. The only difference is the gluing and folding sequence.

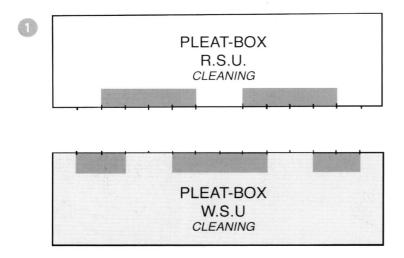

1   Cut a piece of latex 14 x 5cm (5½ x 2in). Mark out the gluing sequence with a felt-tip pen. Clean both seam allowances of the piece to be pleated.

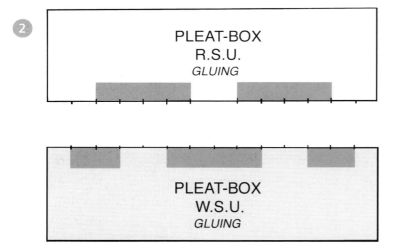

2   Use a 2cm (¾in) spatula to glue the right side. Allow the glue to dry, then turn the piece over and glue the wrong side, as marked.

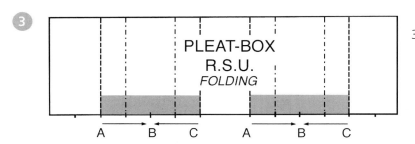

3 With R.S.U., bring points A to B and then C to B. Make sure the folds are at right angles, repositioning them if they are not.

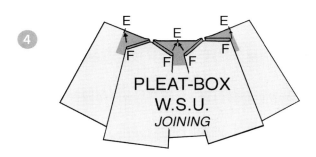

4 Turn the work over and with W.S.U., join points F to E, thus creating the box pleat.

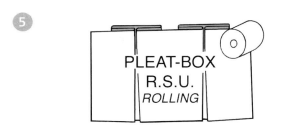

5 Roll all the glued areas firmly.

Chapter 3
Openings and closings

Although latex is a stretch fabric, it is essential to know how to create openings for both practical and aesthetic reasons. The following are the most common types in use.

Press-stud closing

If you try to put press-stud fastenings into garment-weight latex without any added support, the stud hole will stretch under the slightest pressure and the stud will quickly pop out. With this method, woven tape or fabric adheres to the latex along the opening, stopping it from stretching, and forming a solid anchor.

1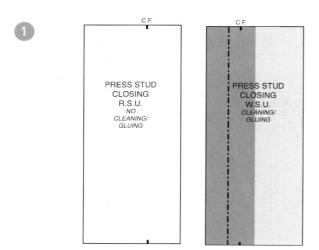

1 Cut a pair of practice fronts, approximately 8 x 16cm (3 x 6½in). The right side needs no cleaning or gluing. For this sample we are going to make a button wrap 2cm (¾in) wide, which should accommodate a standard press stud with a 1.5cm (⅝in) cap. With W.S.U., clean and glue a strip down each C.F., 4cm (1⅝in) wide from top to bottom. On each piece, mark the C.F. notch 2.5cm (1in) in from the seam edge. As a folding guide you can draw a line parallel to the C.F. and 1cm (⅜in) away from it.

2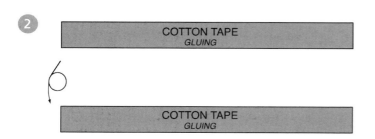

2 Cut two lengths of cotton tape, each 1.5cm (⅝in) wide and the same length as the C.F. Alternatively, it is possible to use strips of any tightly-woven fabric, such as calico, if there is no tape available. Glue these two strips on both sides.

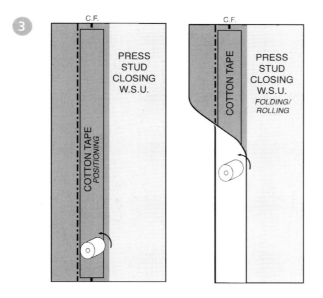

3 Lay the tape strips on the C.F. of both pieces and roll firmly.

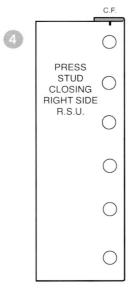

4 Begin to fold back the button wrap and roll firmly. The two fronts are now ready to take press-stud fastenings.

Lacing

Inserting eyelets of the type used for lacing into latex garments produces the same problem as press studs – under pressure, they will easily pop out of the garment. Fortunately, the woven tape or fabric anchor is sufficiently robust to withstand tight lacing. Follow the instructions as above, but with one small pattern-cutting difference: a laced opening does not have a button wrap and needs to meet edge to edge. It is therefore necessary to make your C.F. or C.B the fold line, or the garment will be too big.

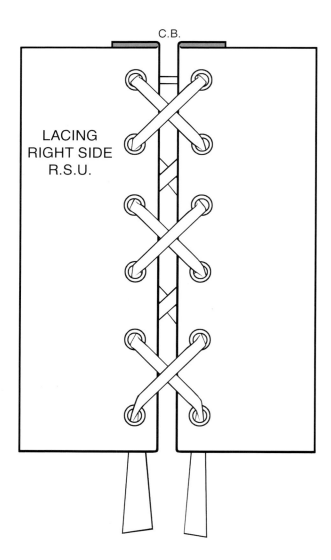

Making a
Simple Seam

1
Tools and
equipment

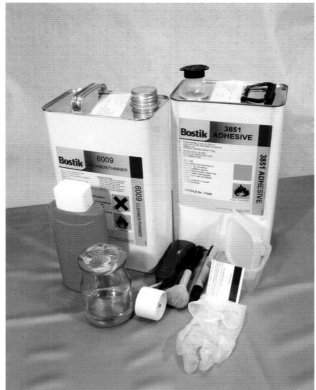

2
Arrange pieces

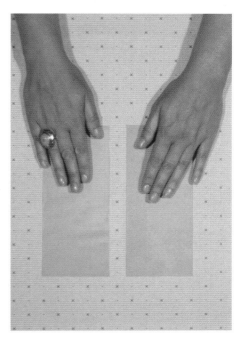

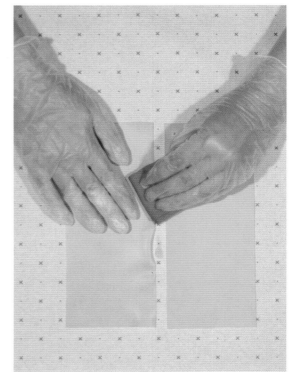

3
Clean latex with thinner

4

Allow cleaning
thinner to dry

5

Glue first seam

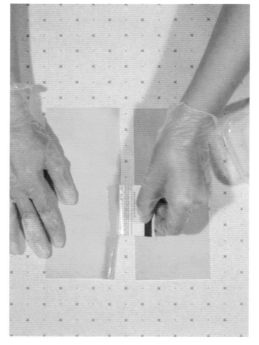

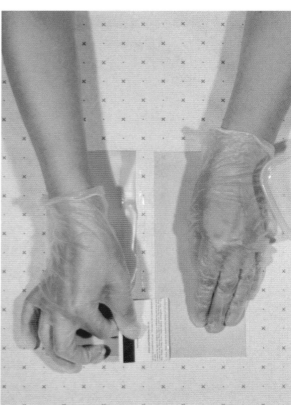

Glue second seam

6

7

Allow glue
to dry

8

Begin to join the seams

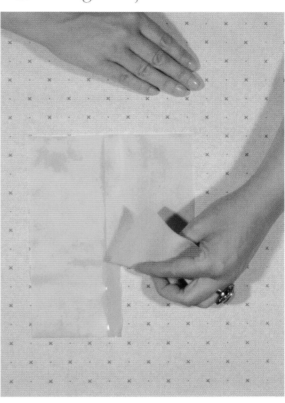

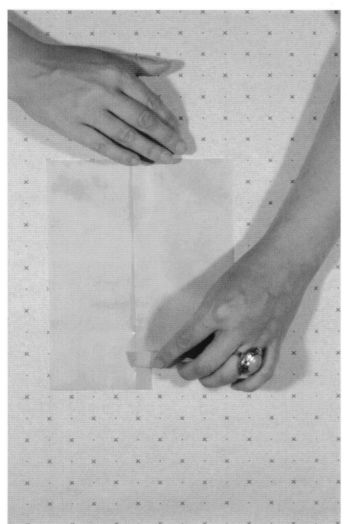

9

Join seams in the
middle and end

10
Use roller to seal seam

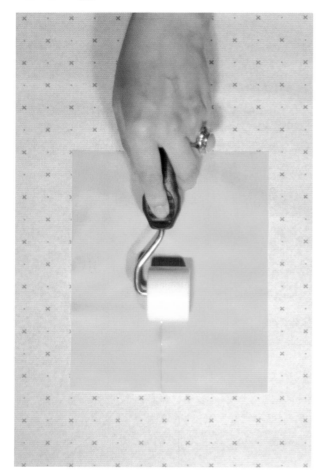

11
Talc seam

12
Brush away
residue of talc

Making a Hem

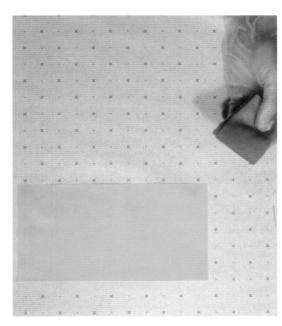

1 Clean latex

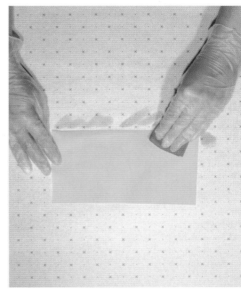

2 Start to glue

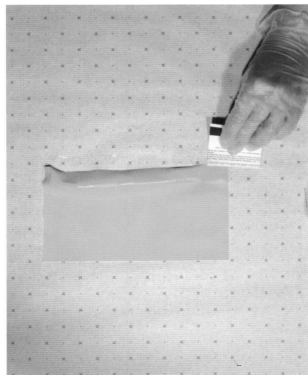

3 Complete gluing

4 Start to hem

5

Use roller at
mid hem

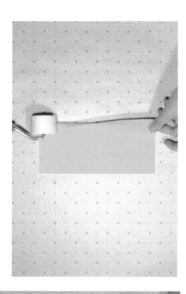

6

Finish hem
with roller

7

Finished
hem

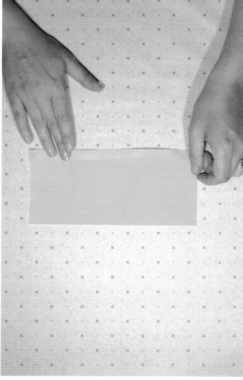

8

Talc hem

9

Brush away
residue of talc

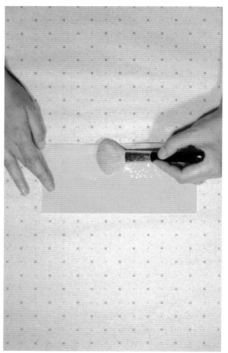

Cowl neck black latex mini dress showing how latex can be draped to produce a highly dramatic look.

Full-length black T-shirt dress.

Jade green latex dress.

Silver latex halter-neck waistcoat with matching tube skirt.

The dress features a cowl neck and edge binding.

The waistcoat uses tie-closing, and the fishtail skirt is a simple adaptation of a tube skirt.

Bubblegum pink bomber jacket and turquoise hipster flared pants. The jacket uses gathering to produce the blouson effect.

This is a lengthened version of the simple T-shirt dress.

Ivory latex 'Western' shirt-dress with silver latex diamond motif.

Appliqué, fringing and
tie-closing are combined in the dress.

Zip (zipper) insertion

This is the simplest way of inserting a zip (zipper).

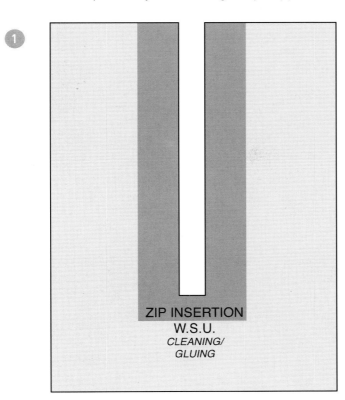

1 Take a small nylon zip and measure the length and width of the teeth. Add 4mm (¼in) to the width measurement. This will give you the size of the channel that needs to be cut in either the C.F. or C.B. of the garment. Cut a piece of latex big enough to accommodate your zip and cut the channel out of the middle. (Should you be making the Panel Dress or any garment in which the zip falls between two seams, remember to halve the zip width measurement and cut this halved measurement from each side.) With W.S.U., clean and glue a 2cm (¾in) strip around the zip channel.

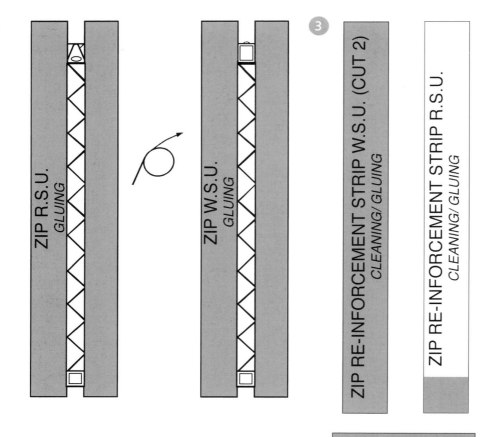

2 ZIP R.S.U. *GLUING*

ZIP W.S.U. *GLUING*

3 ZIP RE-INFORCEMENT STRIP W.S.U. (CUT 2) *CLEANING/ GLUING*

ZIP RE-INFORCEMENT STRIP R.S.U. *CLEANING/ GLUING*

ZIP RE-INFORCEMENT
STRIP W.S.U.

2   Glue webbing tape on both long edges
    of the zip.

3   Cut two reinforcement strips of latex
    the length of the zip tape x 1.5cm ($^5/_8$in)
    and one strip 4cm x 1.5cm ($1^1/_2$in x
    $^5/_8$in). With W.S.U., clean and glue the
    entire length of all the strips. Allow to
    dry, then turn the two longer strips over
    and clean and glue a 1.5cm ($^5/_8$in)
    square at one end of each.

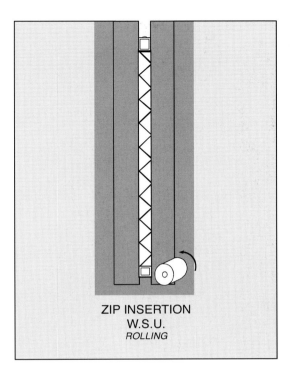

ZIP INSERTION
W.S.U.
ROLLING

4   With W.S.U., place the zip exactly
    over the channel in the main
    piece and roll firmly. Make sure
    there is still a glued section
    around the zip wide enough to
    accommodate the reinforcement
    strips.

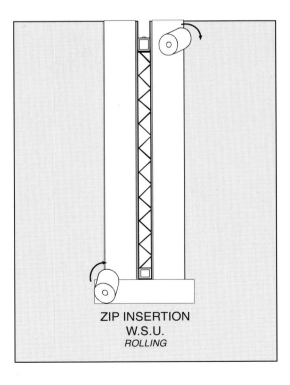

ZIP INSERTION
W.S.U.
ROLLING

5   Place the two long strips down
    over the zip and over the
    remainder of the glued section.
    Roll firmly and place the last strip
    on the bottom of the zip tape so
    that the zip is entirely encased.
    Roll firmly.

Tie closing

Ties work very well in latex garments, as they are both decorative and functional.

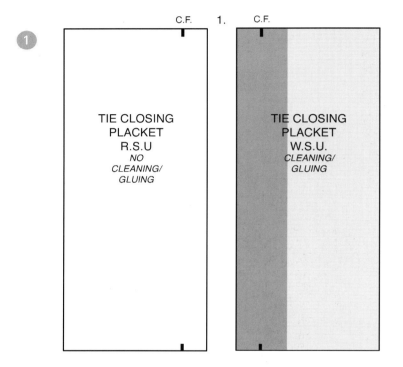

1 Cut two pieces of latex approximately 8 x 18cm (3 x 7in) for the front placket. Clean and glue a 2.5cm (1in) strip down both C.F.s. Mark the C.F.s with a felt-tip pen at top and bottom.

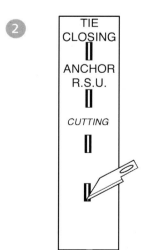

2 Cut a further two strips 3 x 13cm (1¹/₄ x 5in) for the tie anchor and 8 strips, 2 x 16cm (³/₄ x 6in) for the ties. Take the tie anchors, mark the top of the tie positions with a pen and cut vertical slits with a craft knife or scalpel. Each slit should be a fraction longer than the finished width of the ties, in this instance 1cm (³/₈in).

3 TIE CLOSING (CUT 8), TIE PIECE W.S.U.
CLEANING/ GLUING

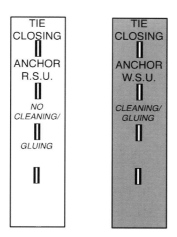

TIE CLOSING ANCHOR R.S.U.
NO CLEANING/ GLUING

TIE CLOSING ANCHOR W.S.U.
CLEANING/ GLUING

3 With W.S.U. clean and glue the tie anchors and the ties.

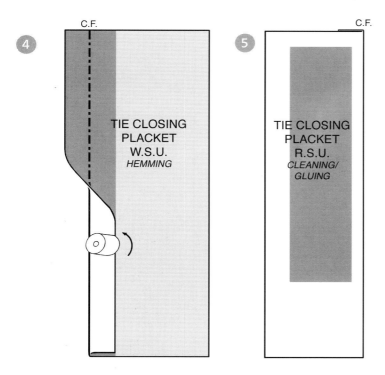

C.F.

TIE CLOSING PLACKET W.S.U.
HEMMING

C.F.

TIE CLOSING PLACKET R.S.U.
CLEANING/ GLUING

4 With W.S.U. start to hem each placket, making the C.F. the fold line. Roll firmly.

5 With each placket R.S.U., clean and glue a rectangle the same measurement as each tie anchor, ie. 3 x 13cm (1¼ x 5in).

TIE PIECE W.S.U.
HEMMING

TIE PIECE R.S.U.

6 Fold the ties in half and press with the roller as if you are hemming them.

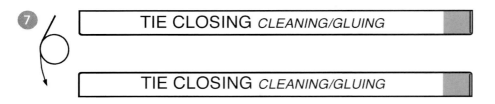

7 With the W.S.U., clean and glue a section 1cm ($^3/_8$in) long at the end of all 8 ties. Turn over and repeat this process.

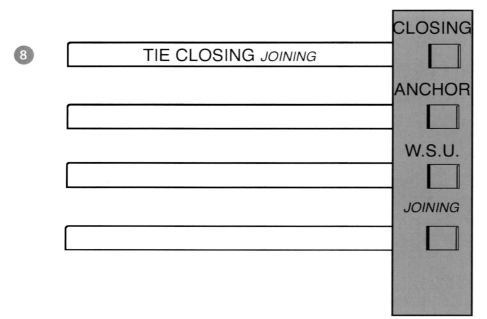

8 Insert one tie into each cut slit of each tie anchor, making sure that the ties lie at right angles to the anchors. You should have a matching pair (see 9a). Roll over the glued ends of the tie anchors.

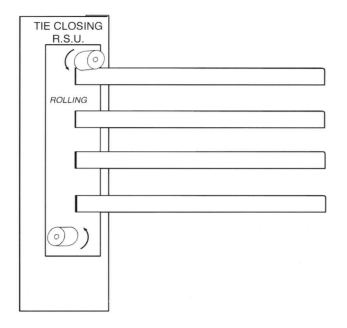

9

TIE CLOSING R.S.U.

ROLLING

9   With the placket and the ties R.S.U. lay the tie anchor over the glued rectangle; make sure the position is correct and roll firmly.

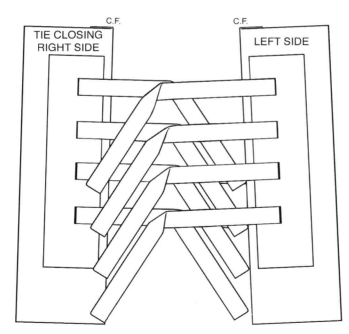

9a

C.F.   C.F.

TIE CLOSING RIGHT SIDE   **LEFT SIDE**

Chapter 4
Embellishments

When designing with latex, the silhouette created does not always convey the original idea adequately, and it is useful to be able to embellish a garment, thus achieving the maximum effect. It is exciting to be able to combine colours, textures and processes, and the following versatile and effective techniques provide virtually limitless scope for the imaginative designer.

Screen printing

It is possible to screen print latex. Many companies offer this service; however I recommend Four D Rubber Ltd. (see Suppliers, page 102) for this process as they are already familiar with the latex sheeting and know the correct way to treat it. There is also the added advantage of being able to buy the raw material and have it processed in the same location.

Heat pleating

Latex sheeting responds quite well to this process. Although the pleats created are not as crisp as they would be in cotton, silk or wool, they still look effective and the process can take the labour out of making pleats by hand.

Appliqué

Appliqué can take almost any form, from military and animal stripes to any symbol you care to think of. For this example I have chosen a series of diamond shapes.

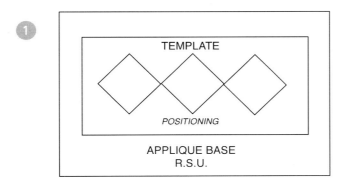

1   Take a rectangle of sturdy card or pattern plastic, and cut a stencil template of the design you wish to make. This will be used as a template for the glue sequence on the main garment (appliqué base). Either use a cut-out piece from the template, or make a separate appliqué template of the diamond shape to mark and cut out the appliqué pieces from a contrasting colour of latex.

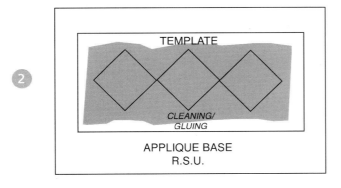

2   Lay the stencil template over the latex sheeting, which should be facing R.S.U. Clean the unmasked area and glue by loading your tool and sliding it firmly across the template. Be careful not to go beyond the template, as this is the right side of the garment.

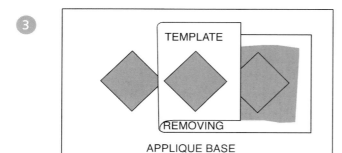

3 Carefully peel the template away from the sheeting and check that the glue has gone into all the corners of the design. If it has not, use a very narrow spatula to fill in any spaces. You want each appliqué piece to be stuck down entirely when finished, otherwise it may peel off at a later stage.

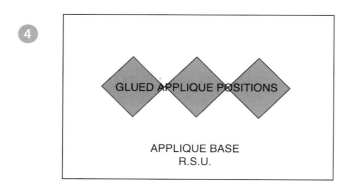

4 Allow the glued sections to dry thoroughly.

APPLIQUE PIECES
CLEANING/GLUING

5. With W.S.U. clean and glue the appliqué pieces.

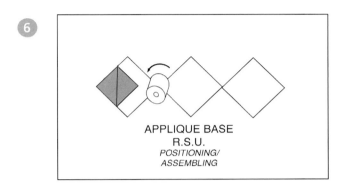

APPLIQUE BASE
R.S.U.
POSITIONING/
ASSEMBLING

6. When dry, gently position the pieces exactly over the glued sections and roll firmly.

Glitter appliqué

For a dazzling effect, prepare a regular stencil appliqué template and use it to apply glue to the latex (main garment). Choose a good-quality fine-grain glitter that does not contain any metal particles and scatter the glued areas generously with it. Roll over the area and brush away any surplus.

Piping

This is a good way of emphasizing an interesting seam or design line, for example, across the bust or down a side seam. It is often made in a contrasting colour to the main garment for even more of an effect. It must be noted that once piping has been inserted the seam will no longer stretch.

1

> **PIPING CASING**
> **R.S.U.**
> *CLEANING/GLUING*

2

> **PIPING CASING**
> **W.S.U.**
> *CLEANING/GLUING*

1 Measure the circumference of your piping cord as these vary in thickness. Keep a note of this measurement. Cut a piece of latex approximately 15cm (6in) long and the circumference of the piping plus 2cm (³/₄in). With R.S.U., clean and glue two 1cm (³/₈in) strips down each long edge of the piping casing as in the diagram. Allow to dry.

2 With W.S.U., clean and glue the entire piece.

44

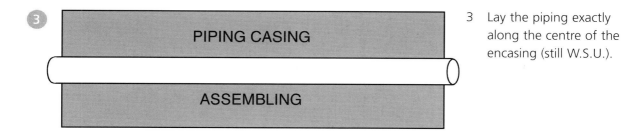

③

PIPING CASING

ASSEMBLING

3 Lay the piping exactly along the centre of the encasing (still W.S.U.).

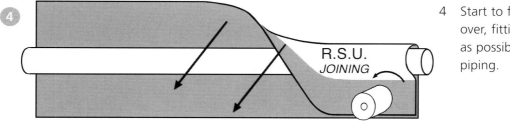

④

R.S.U.
JOINING

4 Start to fold the latex over, fitting it as tightly as possible around the piping.

45

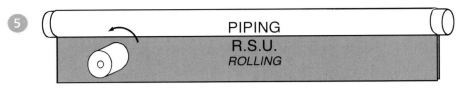

5 Roll the seam allowances firmly together along the piping so that it is completely encased.

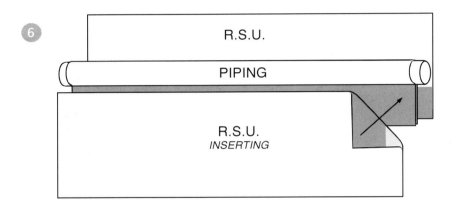

6 Prepare two pieces of latex as for a simple seam (see pages 16-17). Insert the piping by laying it along the glued seam allowance of one piece. Roll the piping to the underside piece as in the diagram. Next position the topside over the piping seam allowance to complete the insertion. Roll once again.

Fringing

Fringing is a lovely way to add theme and character to a garment. Once cut, the strips of latex sit well on the garment and create a lot of movement.

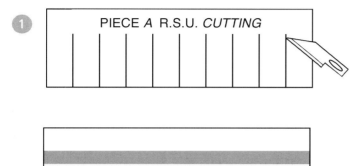

1   Cut one piece of latex approximately 12 x 4cm (5 x 1½in) and another 12 x 6cm (5 x 2½in). On the first piece, mark the fringing with a felt pen, making a series of parallel lines. Do not mark all the way to the top, but leave about 8mm ($^5/_{16}$in) unmarked, for the seam allowance. Use scissors or a scalpel to cut the fringing. On piece B, with R.S.U., clean and glue an 8mm ($^5/_{16}$in) horizontal strip about a quarter of the way down.

2   With W.S.U., clean and glue an 8mm ($^5/_{16}$in) strip across the top of piece A.

3   Lay piece A over piece B and roll firmly.

A curved frill

This type of frill has a different look to the example of gathering shown earlier (see pages 24-25). It is not really used as an integral part of the garment, more as surface decoration. The technique can be used to make lovely 1950s-style frills on bikini bottoms or can be used to great effect around a neckline or a hem.

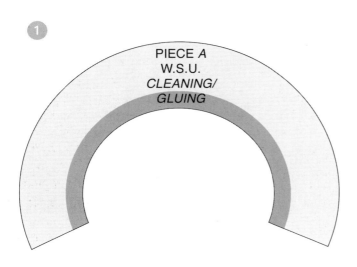

1 Mark and cut out a rectangle (piece B) measuring 18 x 6cm (7 x 2½in), to which the frill is applied. Draw two concentric circles so that you create piece A with the desired depth of the frill, in this case 3cm (1¼in). The measurement of the inner curve of piece A should be the same as the width of piece B (here, 18cm/7in). With W.S.U. clean and glue an 8mm (⁵/₁₆in) strip around the inside of piece A.

②

PIECE *B*
R.S.U.
CLEANING/
GLUING

2 With R.S.U. clean and glue an 8mm (⁵/₁₆in) strip about a quarter of the way down piece B.

③

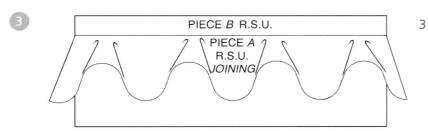

PIECE *B* R.S.U.

PIECE *A*
R.S.U.
JOINING

3 Pick up piece A and turn it over. The glued curved seam has to become 'straight' so that it can be attached to piece B and create the frill. This might seem impossible when first looking at it; with some very gentle manipulation, however, you will discover how easy it is to achieve. Once you are happy with the frill, roll the seam firmly.

Boning

This technique is probably the most difficult to master, especially as it is generally used on curved seams. As with all the processes in this book, accuracy is the key to a successful outcome.

Traditionally, boning is used for corsets and dresses, the aim being to pull the figure into a desired structural shape. I have also seen it used in belts and, in miniature, for decorative neck braces.

PIECE *A*
R.S.U.
CLEANING/
GLUING

1   Clean and glue pieces A and B in the same way as for a simple seam (see pages 16-17).

PIECE *B*
W.S.U.
CLEANING/
GLUING

PIECE *A*
W.S.U.
JOINING

PIECE *B*
W.S.U.

2   With W.S.U., join piece A to piece B.

3 BONING CHANNEL W.S.U. *CLEANING/GLUING*

4

PIECE *A*
W.S.U.
CLEANING/
GLUING

PIECE *B*
W.S.U.

3 Cut the boning casing. This should measure the width of the boning plus 2cm ($^3/_4$in), by the length of the seam. With W.S.U., clean and glue two 8mm ($^5/_{16}$in) strips down each long side of the boning casing and an 8mm ($^5/_{16}$in) strip across one end of it.

4 With W.S.U., clean and glue two 8mm ($^5/_{16}$in) strips down each side of the seam and one 8mm ($^5/_{16}$in) strip across one end of the seam. The seam itself must remain glue-free, or it will be impossible to insert the boning later.

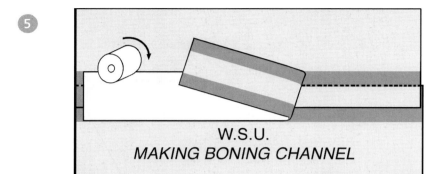

5 (circled)

MAKING BONING CHANNEL

5　Make the boning channel by laying the boning casing over the glued strips around the seam. Accuracy is vital here, as you want to create a channel free from obstructions.

6 (circled)

BONING

6　Cut a piece of boning 3cm (1¼in) shorter than the seam you are working on. This is to give you space to turn the hem at each end of the seam. Use a pair of scissors to 'round' the ends of the bone to prevent it cutting through the latex and tearing the garment. If the boning feels a bit sharp, use a fine piece of glasspaper or an emery board to smooth it down.

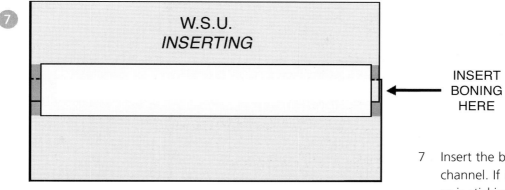

7

INSERT BONING HERE ←

7   Insert the boning into the channel. If it is a tight fit or is sticking, take the boning aside and either spray it with a little silicone or dust it with talcum powder. Replace the boning. With W.S.U., clean and glue a 2.5cm (1in) strip for the hem along the end at which you inserted the boning.

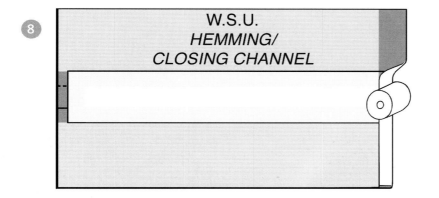

8

8   Hem this and you will find that at the same time you are closing the boning channel.

Latex clothes

Choosing styles and adapting patterns

Almost any style of garment can be adapted for the medium of latex. The many properties of latex lend themselves equally well to a long and flowing evening gown as to a shirt or a tight mini skirt.

If you wish to make any of the items that follow in this section, I suggest that you find simple fabric patterns in the correct size. In general, I recommend that to begin with you use commercial patterns designed for stretch materials, as these rarely possess any darts or fitting lines, the simple shapes being excellent for practice pieces.

The main rule to remember when adapting commercial patterns is that the seam allowances will need to be changed. On a regular sewn garment the standard seam allowance is usually 1cm ($^3/_8$in). I have already established that a glued seam is constructed by overlapping, the standard width of the overlap being 8mm ($^5/_{16}$in). This measurement is arrived at because it combines flexibility of joining shaped seams with the minimum seam allowance required for the strength to hold a garment together. In a fabric garment, the seam allowances are effectively not part of the overall measurement of the finished garment, but on a latex garment, the (overlapped) seam allowance remains part of the overall width. To allow for this, you should therefore cut any pattern piece designed for a fabric garment to the finished size of the piece (in other words, without fabric seam allowances) plus 4mm ($^1/_6$in) along each seam line or half the width of the finished overlapped seam).

Should you want to construct a garment with a dart, cut away any excess fabric within the dart so that you are left with seam allowance of 2mm (1/8in) at the narrowest part and 4mm (5/16in) at the widest.

Sometimes zips (zippers) can be eliminated so that a garment becomes a 'pull-on', as with the Skirt and the Simple Trousers.

Any inserted pockets that appear on patterns, for example, in the front of jeans or in the side seam of a skirt, should also either be eliminated or changed into patch pockets. These pocket bags, however, tend to look very bulky and functional and are not really in keeping with the dramatic and theatrical look that you are trying to achieve with a latex garment. If the design requires one, it is always possible to create a faux pocket with the use of appliqué.

There is no difference in the construction where sizes are concerned; all sizes are made in exactly the same way.

Simple skirt

Cleaning and gluing

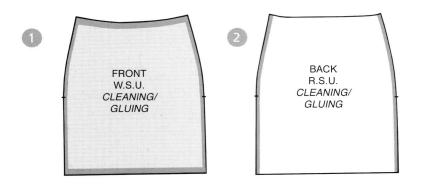

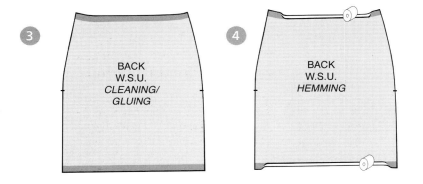

1 Front: with W.S.U., clean and glue an 8mm ($^5/_{16}$in) strip down each of the side seams and a 2 ($^3/_4$in) strip along the top and bottom hems.

2 Back: with R.S.U., clean and glue an 8mm ($^5/_{16}$in) strip down each of the side seams.

3 Back: with W.S.U., clean and glue a 2cm ($^3/_4$in) strip along the top and bottom hems.

4 Back: with W.S.U., start rolling the 1cm ($^3/_8$in) bottom hem 2cm ($^3/_4$in) from one side finishing 2cm ($^3/_4$in) before the other side. Repeat for the waist hem.

5 Front: with R.S.U. repeat the hemming process as above.

Joining

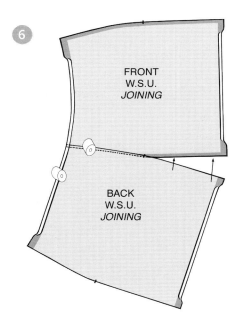

6 Turn both pieces W.S.U. and start to join the side seams by overlapping the back seam allowance over the front. Gently work your way over the curved hip shaping. If you find that you have to stretch it slightly to make the notches match, stretch the front piece a little to compensate. It is important to roll gently, so that if the seam allowance is not correct the seam can be easily pulled apart and redone. Roll the seam firmly and complete the left waist and bottom hems.

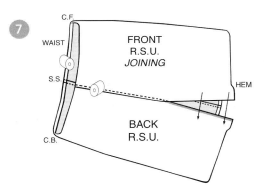

7 Arrange the skirt as in the diagram and complete the right side seam.

8 With the roller complete the right waist and bottom hems (8b).

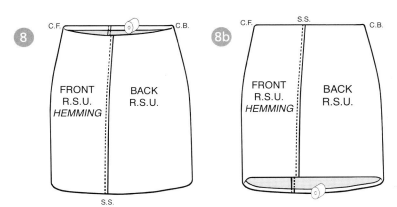

Panel skirt

This is a variation on the simple skirt, but incorporates a little more shaping. A feature can be made of this style by using panels of differing colours or putting a flare into the hem.

Cleaning and gluing

1 With R.S.U., clean and glue an 8mm ($^5/_{16}$in) strip down one side of all the panels.

2 With W.S.U., clean and glue an 8mm ($^5/_{16}$in) strip down the opposite side of each panel. Clean and glue a 2cm ($^3/_4$in) strip along the top and bottom hems.

Hemming, joining and finishing

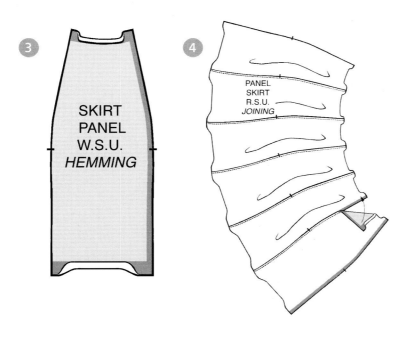

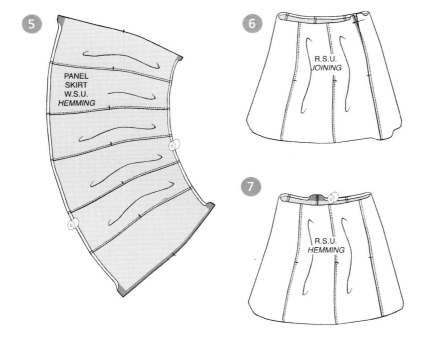

3 Start 2cm (³⁄₄in) from the side seam and with the roller make a 1cm (³⁄₈in) turning at the top and bottom of each panel, finishing 2cm (³⁄₄in) from the other seam.

4 Start to join one panel to another until all six panels are joined as in the illustration. Roll each seam firmly.

5 Flip the whole skirt over carefully and complete all the hems of the joined panels.

6 Join the last two panels together. Roll the seam firmly.

7 Finish the last top and bottom hems to complete the skirt.

Vest top

Cleaning and gluing

FRONT
W.S.U.
*CLEANING/
GLUING*

BACK
W.S.U.
*CLEANING/
GLUING*

FRONT
R.S.U.
*NO
CLEANING/
GLUING*

BACK
R.S.U.
*CLEANING/
GLUING*

1 Front: with W.S.U., clean and glue a 2cm (^{3}/4in) strip around the armholes, neck and hem. Clean and glue an 8mm (^{5}/16in) strip down each side seam and across both shoulder seams. If the curves around the armholes and neck are very tight, reduce the seam allowance to 1cm (^{3}/8in).

2 Back: with W.S.U., clean and glue a 2cm (^{3}/4in) strip around armholes, neck and hem. As with above, reduce the seam allowance if the curves are tight.

3 Front: R.S.U., no cleaning or gluing.

4 Back: R.S.U., clean and glue an 8mm (^{5}/16in) strip down each side seam and across both shoulder seams.

Hemming and joining

FRONT
W.S.U.
HEMMING

BACK
W.S.U.
HEMMING

5   Front: start rolling the neck hem, which is 1 cm ($^3/_8$in) deep, 2cm ($^3/_4$in) from one side and finish 2cm ($^3/_4$in) from the other side. Repeat for the armholes and waist hem.

6   Back: repeat as for the front.

BACK
W.S.U.
*JOINING+
HEMMING*

FRONT
W.S.U.
*JOINING+
HEMMING*

7   Turn both front and back W.S.U. and join the shoulder seams. Finish the adjoining armhole and neck hems with the roller.

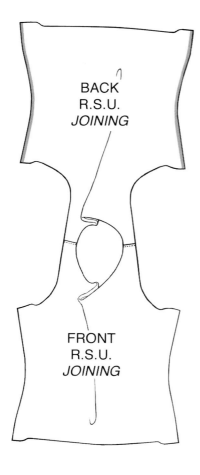

BACK
R.S.U.
JOINING

FRONT
R.S.U.
JOINING

8   Turn garment R.S.U.

9   Arrange garment as
    displayed in the diagram
    and join left side seam.
    Finish underarm and
    waist hem with roller.

FRONT
R.S.U.
JOINING

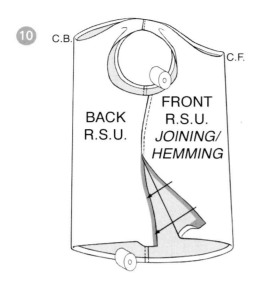

C.B.

C.F.

BACK
R.S.U.

FRONT
R.S.U.
*JOINING/
HEMMING*

10 Arrange garment as displayed in the diagram and join right side seam.

11 Finish underarm and waist hem with roller.

FRONT
R.S.U.
HEMMING

Halter top
Cleaning and gluing
This is a variation on the vest.

1 Front: with W.S.U., clean and glue an 8mm ($^5/_{16}$in) strip down each side seam and on one of the C.B. neck straps. Then clean and glue a 2cm ($^3/_4$in) strip along the bottom hem, the underarms and around the neckline. If the neckline and underarms are really tight curves, reduce the glue strips to 1cm ($^3/_8$in). A smaller turning is easier to make around a sharp curve.

2 Front: with R.S.U., clean and glue the opposite C.B. neck strap.

3 Back: with W.S.U., clean and glue a 2cm ($^3/_4$in) strip along the top and bottom hems. (If you have taken a smaller seam allowance around the underarms on the front, do the same on the top back hem.)

4 Back: with R.S.U., clean and glue an 8mm ($^5/_{16}$in) strip down both of the side seams.

Hemming and joining

5 Front: begin to make a turning 2cm (³/₄in) from the side seams and, using the roller, hem around the underarms. Start 2cm (³/₄in) from the C.B. neck strap and hem all around the neckline, stopping 2cm (³/₄in) short of the other C.B. neck strap.

6 Back: begin to make the top and bottom turnings, starting 2cm (³/₄in) from one side seam and ending 2cm (³/₄in) from the other.

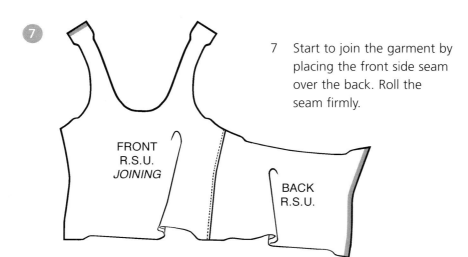

7 Start to join the garment by placing the front side seam over the back. Roll the seam firmly.

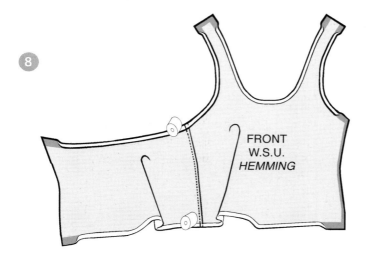

8   Turn the garment over and complete the hem at the top and bottom of the side seam with the roller.

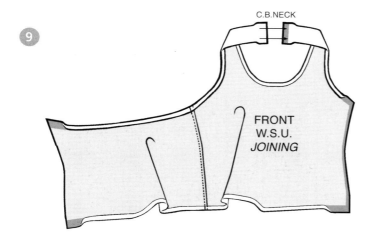

9   Join the C.B. neck straps.

10   C.B.NECK   C.B.NECK

10 Complete the C.B. neck hems with the roller.

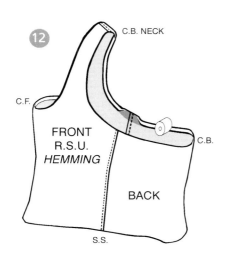

BACK
R.S.U.
JOINING

11 Arrange the garment as illustrated and join the other side seam. Roll firmly.

C.B. NECK

C.F.

FRONT
R.S.U.
HEMMING

C.B.

BACK

S.S.

12 Complete the remaining two hems at the top and bottom of the side seam.

C.B.NECK

FRONT
R.S.U.
HEMMING

Simple trousers
Cleaning and gluing

FRONT LEFT LEG
R.S.U.
*CLEANING/
GLUING*

FRONT RIGHT LEG
R.S.U.
*NO CLEANING
OR GLUING
NEEDED*

FRONT RIGHT LEG
W.S.U.
*CLEANING/
GLUING*

FRONT LEFT LEG
W.S.U.
*CLEANING/
GLUING*

1 Front, left leg: with R.S.U., clean and glue an 8mm ($^5/_{16}$in) strip down the centre front.

2 Front, right leg: R.S.U. needs no cleaning or gluing.

3 Front, right leg: with W.S.U., clean and glue an 8mm ($^5/_{16}$in) strip down the centre front, the side seam, and the inside leg seam. Clean and glue a 2cm ($^3/_4$in) strip around the waist and hem.

4 Front, left leg: when dry, turn the piece over and, with W.S.U., clean and glue an 8mm ($^5/_{16}$in) strip down the side and the inside leg. Clean and glue a 2cm ($^3/_4$in) strip around the waist and hem.

C.B.

BACK RIGHT LEG
R.S.U.
CLEANING/
GLUING

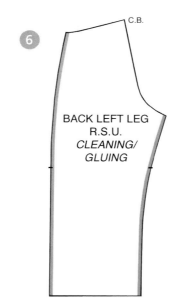

C.B.

BACK LEFT LEG
R.S.U.
CLEANING/
GLUING

C.B.

BACK LEFT LEG
W.S.U.
CLEANING/
GLUING

C.B.

BACK RIGHT LEG
W.S.U.
CLEANING/
GLUING

5   Back, right leg: with R.S.U., clean and glue an 8mm ($5/_{16}$in) strip along the centre back, side seam, and inside leg seam.

6   Back, left leg: with R.S.U., clean and glue an 8mm ($5/_{16}$in) strip down the side seam and the inside leg seam.

7   Back, left leg: with W.S.U., clean and glue an 8mm ($5/_{16}$in) strip down the centre back. Clean and glue a 2cm ($3/_4$in) strip around the waist and hem.

8   Back, right leg: with W.S.U., clean and glue a 2cm ($3/_4$in) strip around the waist and the hem.

Hemming and joining

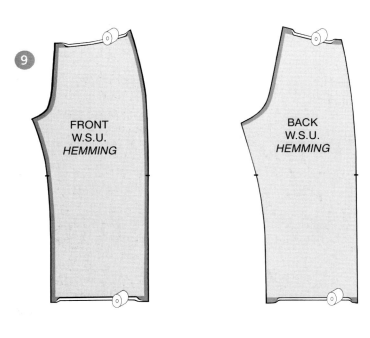

9 Front, right leg: with W.S.U., start a 1cm (³⁄₈in) hem along the waist, 2cm (³⁄₄in) from C.B. and stopping 2cm (³⁄₄in) from the side seam. Repeat the same process for the remaining leg pieces.

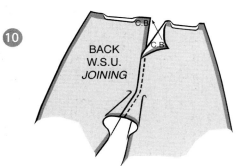

10 Take the two back pieces and, with the W.S.U. and starting at the crotch, overlap the glued strips to form an 8mm (⁵⁄₁₆in) seam, working towards the waist of the C.B.s,. Roll the seam firmly. Take the two front pieces and work in the same way from the crotch to the waist. Again, roll the seam firmly.

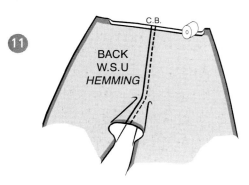

11 Finish the hems on the C.F. and C.B. with the roller.

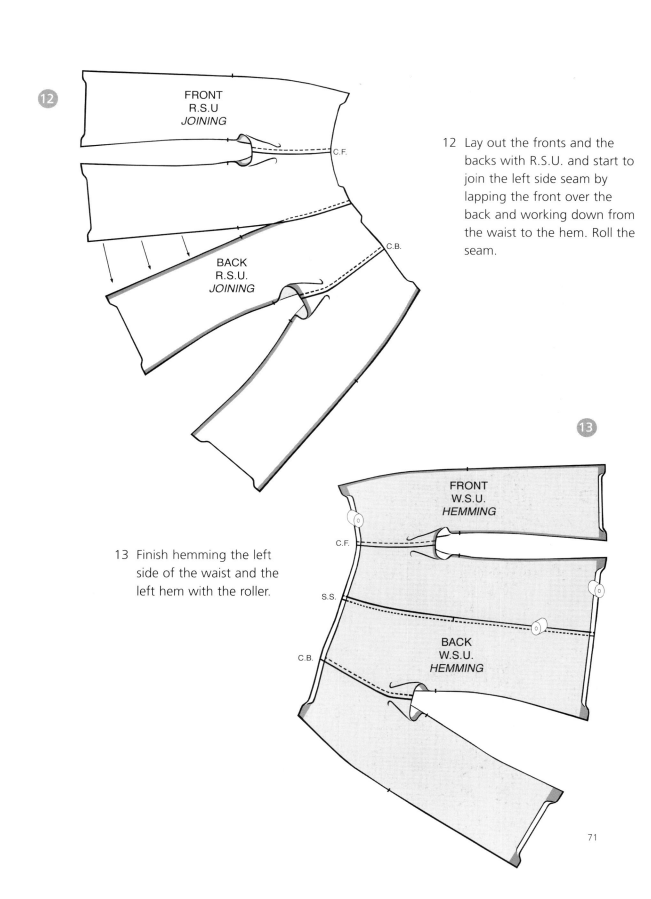

12

FRONT
R.S.U
JOINING

C.F.

BACK
R.S.U.
JOINING

C.B.

12 Lay out the fronts and the backs with R.S.U. and start to join the left side seam by lapping the front over the back and working down from the waist to the hem. Roll the seam.

13 Finish hemming the left side of the waist and the left hem with the roller.

13

FRONT
W.S.U.
HEMMING

C.F.

S.S.

BACK
W.S.U.
HEMMING

C.B.

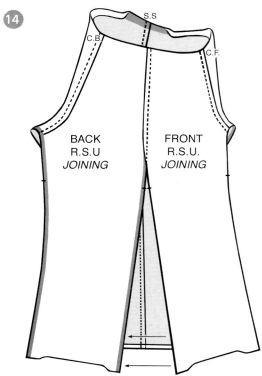

BACK
R.S.U
JOINING

FRONT
R.S.U.
JOINING

S.S

C.B.

C.F.

14 Arrange the garment as displayed in the diagram, and join the right side seam, working from waist to hem. Roll the seam.

15 Finish hemming the right side of the waist and hem with the roller.

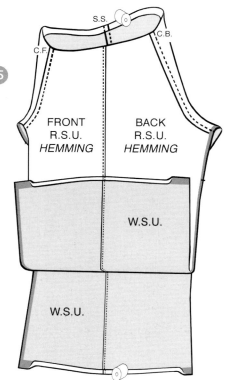

S.S.

C.F.

C.B.

FRONT
R.S.U.
HEMMING

BACK
R.S.U.
HEMMING

W.S.U.

W.S.U.

16 Arrange the garment as
displayed in the diagram and
join the inside leg seam from
crotch to hem on the left leg.
Repeat for the right leg.

17 Close the remaining hems with
the roller.

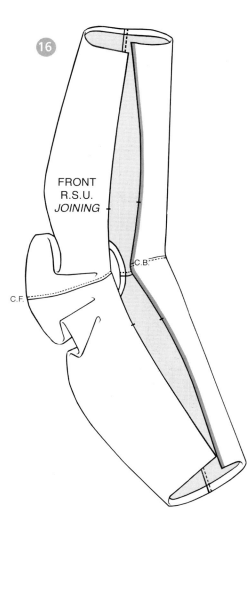

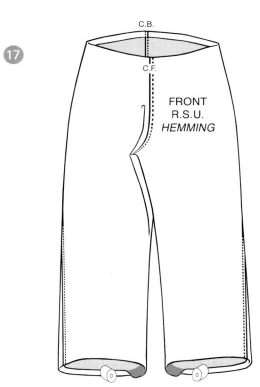

T-shirt

Cleaning and gluing

FRONT
W.S.U.
*CLEANING/
GLUING*

FRONT
R.S.U.
*CLEANING/
GLUING*

BACK
W.S.U.
*CLEANING/
GLUING*

BACK
R.S.U.
*CLEANING/
GLUING*

S.H.N.

SLEEVE
W.S.U.
*CLEANING/
GLUING*

F.N.

S.H.N.

F.N.

SLEEVE
R.S.U.
*CLEANING/
GLUING*

1   Front: with W.S.U., clean and glue an 8mm (⁵⁄₁₆in) strip on the side seams and the shoulder seams. Clean and glue a 2cm (³⁄₄in) strip around the neck and the hem. Allow to dry.

2   Front: with the R.S.U., clean and glue an 8mm (⁵⁄₁₆in) strip around both armholes.

3   Back: with W.S.U., clean and glue a 2cm (³⁄₄in) strip around the neck and the hem. Allow to dry.

4   Back: with the R.S.U., clean and glue an 8mm (⁵⁄₁₆in) strip along the shoulder seams, around both armholes and down the side seams.

5   Sleeves: with W.S.U., clean and glue an 8mm (⁵⁄₁₆in) strip along the top curve of the sleeve and down the front side seam. Clean and glue a 2cm (³⁄₄in) strip along the hem edge.

6   Sleeves: with R.S.U., clean and glue an 8mm (⁵⁄₁₆in) strip down the back of the sleeve side seam.

Hemming and joining

7   Sleeves: with W.S.U., use the roller to hem the sleeves. Start the 1cm (³/₈in) hem 2cm (³/₄in) from one side and finish 2cm (³/₄in) from the other.

8   Front: with W.S.U., use the roller to start a 1cm (³/₈in) hem at the neck. Begin and end 2cm (³/₄in) from the shoulder point. Turn the waist hem in the same way.

9   Back: repeat the above process.

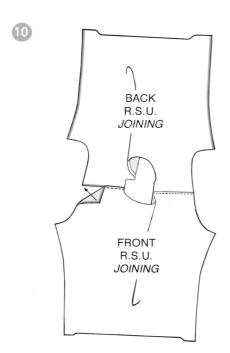

10 BACK
R.S.U.
JOINING

FRONT
R.S.U.
JOINING

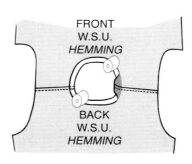

11 FRONT
W.S.U.
HEMMING

BACK
W.S.U.
HEMMING

10 With R.S.U., join the shoulder
seams and roll firmly.

11 Turn over to W.S.U. and finish the
neck hem with the roller.

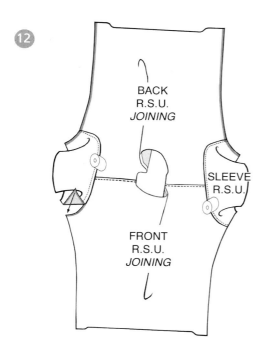

12 BACK
R.S.U.
JOINING

SLEEVE
R.S.U.

FRONT
R.S.U.
JOINING

12 Turn back to R.S.U. and put in the
sleeves by joining the sleeve-head
notch to the shoulder seam,
working towards the underarm at
the back and then to the front.
This ensures that the sleeve is
evenly fitted into the armhole. Roll
over the seams firmly.

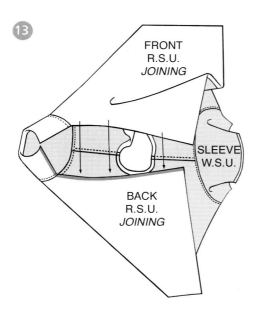

13 Arrange the garment as displayed in the diagram and join the side seam from the sleeve hem to the body hem. Roll seams firmly.

14 Repeat the above process for the other side seam.

15 Finish hems on sleeves and side seams, using the roller.

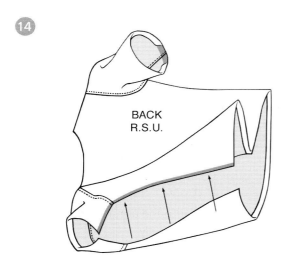

Cowl-neck dress

Cleaning and gluing

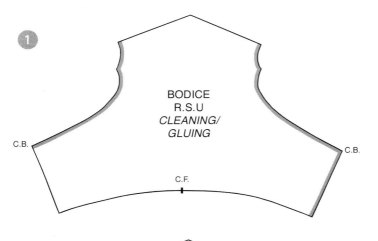

1 Bodice: with R.S.U., clean and glue an 8mm (⁵/₁₆in) strip along the underarm seams and down the right side of the C.B.

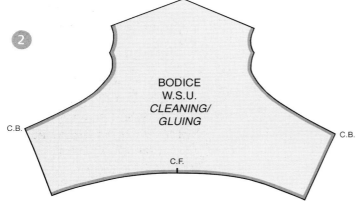

2 Bodice: with W.S.U., clean and glue an 8mm (⁵/₁₆in) strip along the underarm seams, down the left side of the C.B. and around the waist seam.

3 Front skirt: with the W.S.U., clean and glue an 8mm (⁵/₁₆in) strip down each side seam. Clean and glue a 2cm (³/₄in) strip along the hem edge.

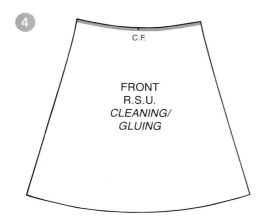

4

C.F.

FRONT
R.S.U.
*CLEANING/
GLUING*

4   Front skirt: with R.S.U., clean and glue an 8mm ($^5/_{16}$in) strip around the waist.

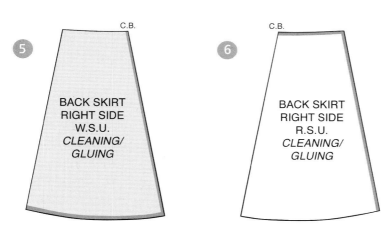

5

C.B.

BACK SKIRT
RIGHT SIDE
W.S.U.
*CLEANING/
GLUING*

6

C.B.

BACK SKIRT
RIGHT SIDE
R.S.U.
*CLEANING/
GLUING*

5 Back skirt, right side: with W.S.U., clean and glue an 8mm ($^5/_{16}$in) strip down the C.B. and a 2cm ($^3/_4$in) strip along the hem.

6 Back skirt, right side: with R.S.U., clean and glue an 8mm ($^5/_{16}$in) strip down the side seam and around the waist edge.

7   Back skirt, left side: with W.S.U., clean and glue a 2cm (³/4in) strip along the hem.

8   Back skirt, left side: with the R.S.U., clean and glue an 8mm (⁵/16in) strip down the C.B., side seam and around the waist.

Note: for the binding halter strap you will need one length of latex 156 x 2cm (62 ¹/2 x ³/4in) cleaned, glued on the wrong side.

Finishing

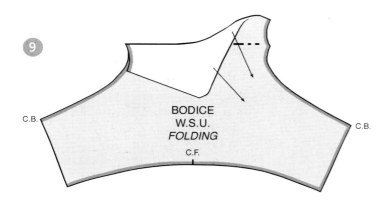

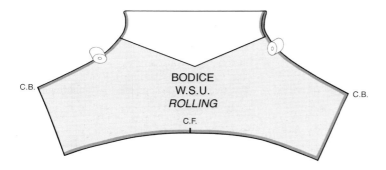

9   Fold the cowl facing down onto the bodice and ensure the glued seams on the wrong side overlap exactly. Use the roller to secure the facing in position.

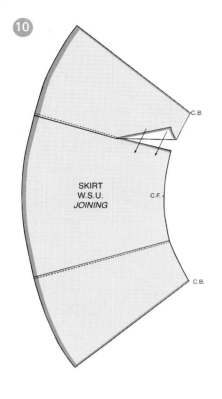

10

SKIRT
W.S.U.
JOINING

C.B.

C.F.

C.B.

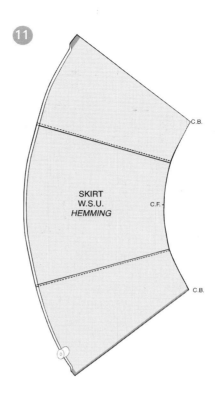

11

SKIRT
W.S.U.
HEMMING

C.B.

C.F.

C.B.

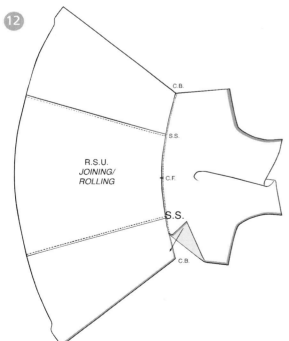

12

R.S.U.
JOINING/
ROLLING

C.B.

S.S.

C.F.

S.S.

C.B.

10 Join the front skirt panels to the back, rolling the seams firmly in place.

11 Start the 1cm (³/₈in) hem, 2cm (³/₄in) from left C.B. and finish 2cm (³/₄in) from the right C.B.

12 Join the bodice to the skirt, starting at the C.F. and working out towards the C.B.s. Roll firmly.

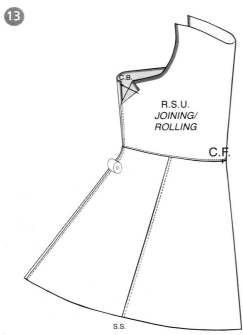

13

R.S.U.
*JOINING/
ROLLING*

C.B.

C.F.

S.S.

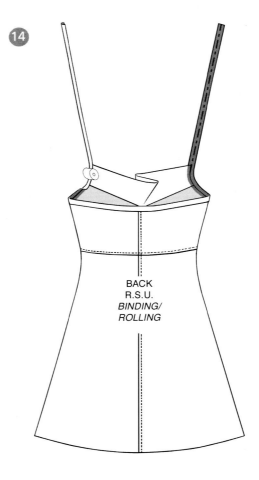

14

BACK
R.S.U.
*BINDING/
ROLLING*

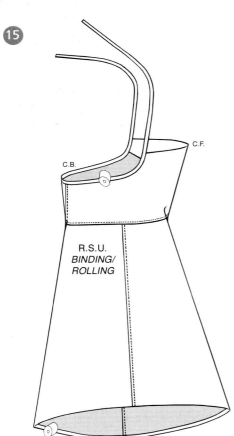

15

C.F.

C.B.

R.S.U.
*BINDING/
ROLLING*

13 Arrange the garment as displayed in the diagram and join the C.B. seams. Finish the C.B. hem with the roller.

14 Take the length of binding and mark a C.B. notch with a light-coloured felt pen halfway along. Start to lay it on the C.B. of the dress, overlapping by 1cm (³⁄₈in). Work towards the front of the cowl and then do the same for the other side.

15 To complete the binding, fold one end over by 1cm (³⁄₈in) so it overlaps itself exactly, and use the roller in one continuous action until you reach the other end of the strap.

Panel dress

Cleaning and gluing

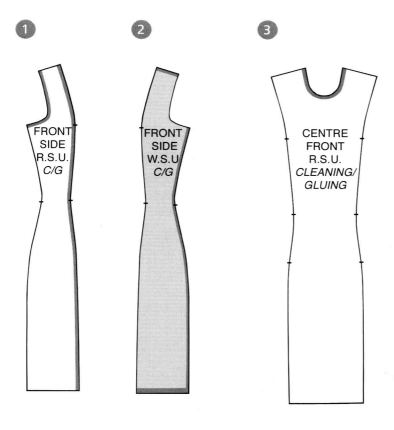

1 Front, sides: with R.S.U., clean and glue an 8mm ($^5/_{16}$in) strip around armholes and down the bust seamline.

2 Front, sides: with W.S.U. clean and glue an 8mm ($^5/_{16}$in) strip along the shoulder seam and down the side seam. Clean and glue a 2cm ($^3/_4$in) strip along the hem edge.

3 C.F. section: with R.S.U., clean and glue an 8mm ($^5/_{16}$in) strip around the neck.

4 C.F.

CENTRE
FRONT
W.S.U.
*CLEANING/
GLUING*

5 BACK
SIDE
W.S.U.
C/G

4 C.F. section: with W.S.U., clean and glue an 8mm (⁵/₁₆in) strip along the shoulders and down the bust seams. Clean and glue a 2cm (³/₄in) strip along the hem edge.

5 Back, sides: with W.S.U., clean and glue a 2.5cm (1in) strip along the hem.

6 Back, sides: with R.S.U., clean and glue an 8mm (⁵/₁₆in) strip along the shoulder, down the side seam and the back-shaping seam.

6 BACK
SIDE
R.S.U.
C/G

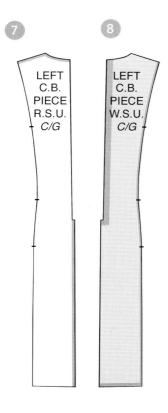

7   C.B. section, left side: with R.S.U., clean and glue an 8mm (⁵⁄₁₆in) strip around the neck, the shoulder, and the lower part of the C.B.

8   C.B. section, left side: with W.S.U. clean and glue a 2cm (³⁄₄in) strip down the upper C.B. (the zip channel) and the hem. Clean and glue an 8mm (⁵⁄₁₆in) seam down the back-shaping seam.

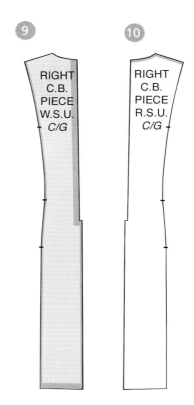

9   C.B. section, right side: with W.S.U., clean and glue a 2cm (³⁄₄in) strip down the C.B. to the bottom of the zip channel, and along the hem. Clean and glue an 8mm (⁵⁄₁₆in) strip down the remainder of the C.B. and the back-shaping seam.

10   C.B. section, right side: with R.S.U., clean and glue an 8mm (⁵⁄₁₆in) strip along the neck and shoulder.

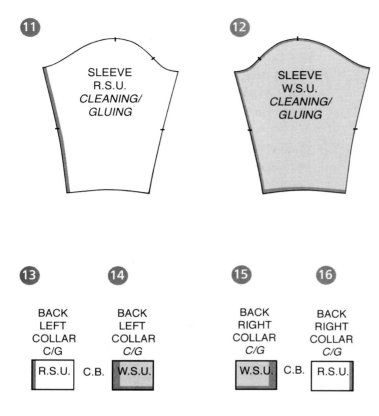

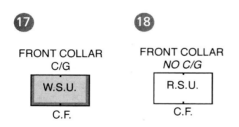

11 Sleeves: with R.S.U., clean and glue an 8mm (⁵/₁₆in) strip down the back side seam.

12 Sleeves: with W.S.U., clean and glue an 8mm (⁵/₁₆in) strip along the top curve of the sleeve and the front side seam. Clean and glue a 2cm (³/₄in) strip along the hem.

13 Collar, back left side: with R.S.U., clean and glue an 8mm (⁵/₁₆in) strip down the side seam.

14 Collar, back left side: with W.S.U. clean and glue a 2cm (³/₄in) strip down the C.B. Clean and glue an 8mm (⁵/₁₆in) strip around the neck seam.

15 Collar, back right side: with W.S.U., clean and glue a 2cm (³/₄in) strip down the C.B. Clean and glue an 8mm (⁵/₁₆in) strip around neck seam.

16 Collar, back right side: with R.S.U., clean and glue an 8mm (⁵/₁₆in) strip down the side seam.

17 Collar, front: with W.S.U., clean and glue an 8mm (⁵/₁₆in) strip down the side seams and the neck seam.

18 Collar, front: R.S.U., no cleaning or gluing.

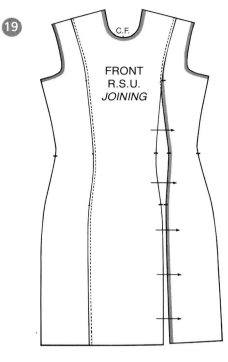

19 Take the C.F. panel and join it to the front side panels, starting at the shoulder and ending at the hem. Take care to match notches. Roll the seams.

20 Take the two C.B. panels and join them from below the zip channel to the hem. Then join to the back side panels, starting at the shoulder and ending at the hem.

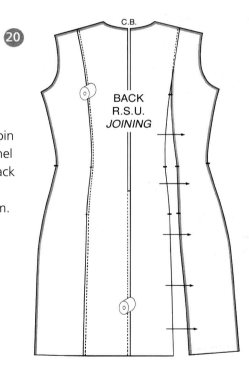

21 Back: turn the joined up back panels W.S.U. and hem the back of the dress with the roller. Start the 1cm (³/₈in) hem 2cm (³/₄in) from one side and finish 2cm (³/₄in) from the other.

22 Sleeves: with W.S.U., hem as above.

23 Front: turn the joined up front panels W.S.U. and hem as above.

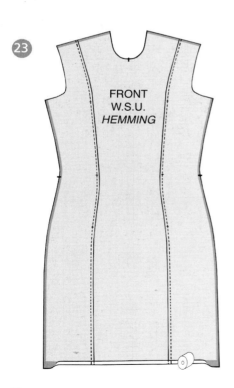

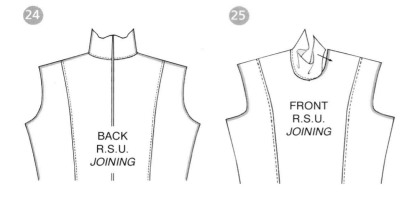

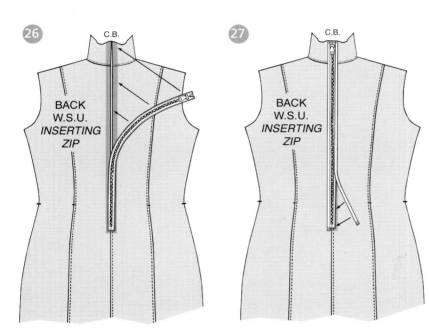

24 Join the two back collar pieces to the left and right back necks. Roll seams.

25 Join the front collar to the front neck of the dress, starting at the C.F. notch and working towards each shoulder in turn. Roll seam.

26 Insert the zip (zipper) by laying it over the zip channel (see page 33 for method for reinforcing and inserting a zip). Roll down the length of the zip on both sides.

27 Lay the 1.5cm ($^5/_8$in) strips down onto the zip. Half of the strip should cover the zip and half should cover the strip of glue on the C.B. Roll firmly.

Joining and finishing

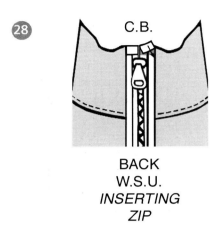

C.B.

**BACK
W.S.U.
*INSERTING
ZIP***

28 Clean and glue the top and bottom of the zip. Place the 1 x 4cm (³/₈ x 1¹/₂in) strips in these positions. When they are rolled they completely seal in the zip and prevent it peeling away from the garment.

29 Turn the front and back R.S.U. and join the shoulder seams and the side collar seams.

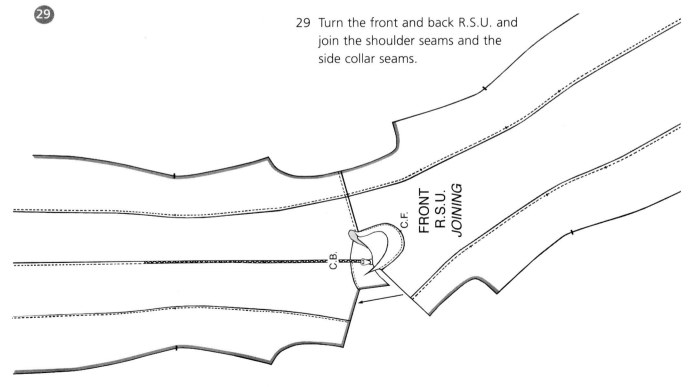

C.F.

C.B.

***FRONT
R.S.U.
JOINING***

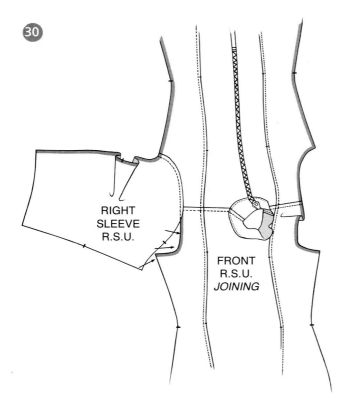

30 RIGHT SLEEVE R.S.U.

FRONT R.S.U. *JOINING*

30 Arrange the garment as displayed in the diagram and join the sleeves, starting at the sleeve-head notch and working towards the underarm.

31 Re-arrange the garment again, as in the diagram, with the back facing up, and join the side seam, continuing up along the sleeve. Repeat the process for the other side seam and sleeve.

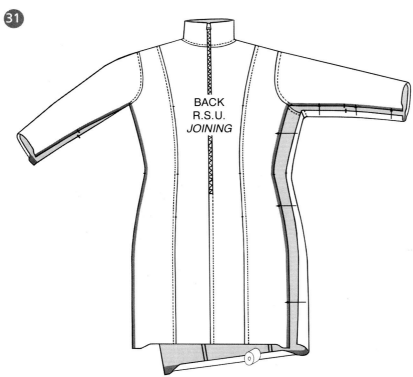

31 BACK R.S.U. *JOINING*

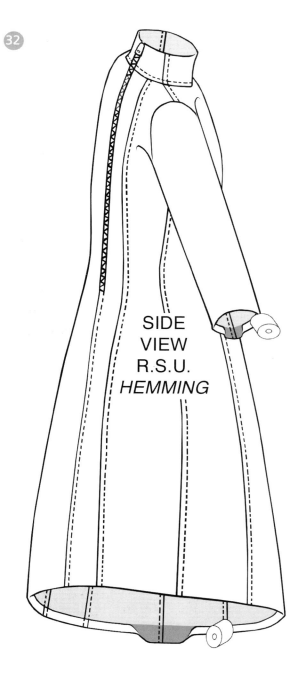

**SIDE
VIEW
R.S.U.
*HEMMING***

32 Finish the hems on the side seams
and the sleeves with the roller.

Corset

Cleaning and gluing

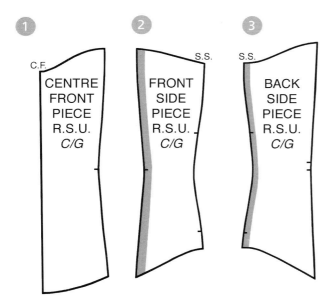

1 C.F. sections: R.S.U., no cleaning or gluing.

2 Front, side sections: with R.S.U., clean and glue an 8mm (5/16in) strip down the bust seam.

3 Back, side sections: with R.S.U., clean and glue an 8mm (5/16in) strip down the side seam.

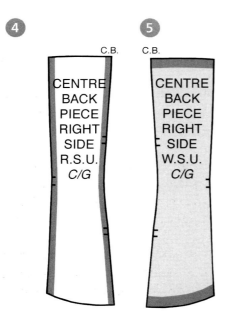

4 C.B. section, right side: with R.S.U., clean and glue an 8mm (⁵/₁₆in) strip down the C.B. and the back-shaping seam.

5 C.B. section, right side: with W.S.U., clean and glue a 2cm (³/₄in) strip along the top and bottom hems.

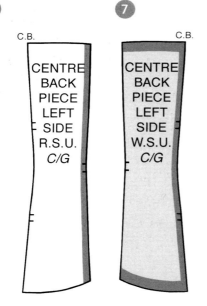

6 C.B. section, left side: with R.S.U., clean and glue an 8mm (⁵/₁₆in) strip down the back-shaping seam.

7 C.B. section, left side: with W.S.U., clean and glue an 8mm (⁵/₁₆in) strip down the C.B. seam. Clean and glue a 2cm (³/₄in) strip along the top and bottom hems.

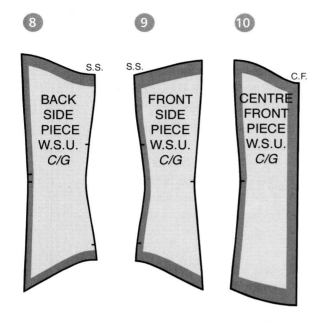

8 Back, side sections: with W.S.U., clean and glue an 8mm ($^5/_{16}$in) strip down the back-shaping seam. Clean and glue a 2cm ($^3/_4$in) strip along the top and bottom hems.

9 Front, side sections: with W.S.U., clean and glue an 8mm ($^5/_{16}$in) strip down the side seam. Clean and glue a 2cm ($^3/_4$in) strip along the top and bottom hems.

10 In order to accommodate two pieces of boning either side of the vertical row of eyelets it is necessary to clean and glue an 8mm ($^5/_{16}$mm) strip down the C.F. with the W.S.U. This measurement is arrived at by adding the width of the two pieces of boning to the width of the eyelets, plus a small margin on either side to encase them all entirely under the facing. The boning and eyelets may vary in size so do check that you have glued a strip wide enough to accommodate all these elements.

11

BONING CASING W.S.U. *C/G*
CUT x 7

12

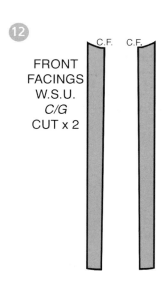

C.F.   C.F.

FRONT
FACINGS
W.S.U.
C/G
CUT x 2

11 Carefully measure the width of your chosen boning. Cut 7 pieces of latex for the boning casing. These should each measure the width of the boning plus 2cm ($^3/_4$in) by the length of the longest vertical seam on the corset. With W.S.U., clean and glue two 8mm ($^5/_{16}$in) strips along the edges of all the boning casing strips.

12 Cut two front facings the length of the C.F. by the width as calculated in step 10 for the glued C.F. section – in this case the measurement is 8mm ($^5/_{16}$mm). With W.S.U., clean and glue.

Joining

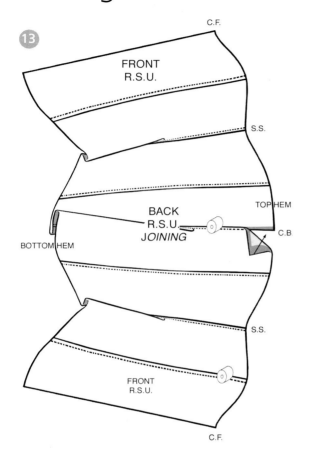

13 Begin to assemble the corset, matching the notches. Make sure that none of the pieces are put in upside-down – at a glance, the pieces are very similar to one another and this is a common mistake. Roll each seam firmly.

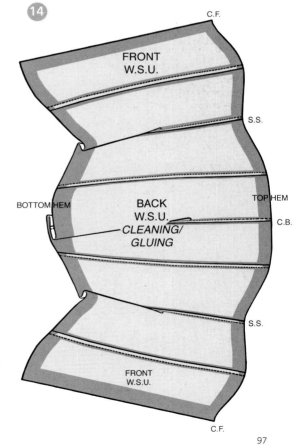

14 Carefully turn the whole piece over, with W.S.U. Clean and glue two 8mm (⁵/₁₆in) strips down each side of every seam, leaving an untreated – neither cleaned nor glued – strip the width of your boning exactly down the middle. This forms the channel down which the boning will be inserted. If there is any glue or thinner in this position it may become impossible to push the boning into place.

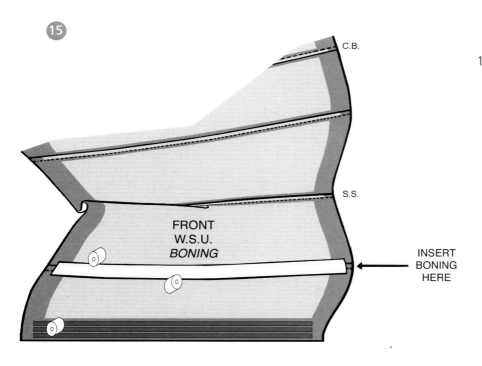

15 Arrange the garment so that one of the C.F.s is immediately in front of you. Lay down the first piece of boning on the C.F. 3cm (⅛in) away from the edge. The boning should start and end 1.5mm (⅝in) from the top and bottom hems, allowing enough room to turn them. Next to the first piece of boning, lay down the strip of fabric or tape and then place the final piece of boning beside that. Roll all these elements firmly, in preparation for the facing. Repeat for the other C.F. Roll firmly, making sure that you also press down on the fabric strip or tape and seal it properly. Create the boning channels by laying the prepared strips over the rest of the corset seams (see page 52) and insert the boning. Lay the front facings over the C.F.s of the corset and roll firmly. Clean and glue the top and bottom of each boning channel. Allow to dry and then hem the corset, making sure that the top and bottom of each boning channel is entirely sealed closed.

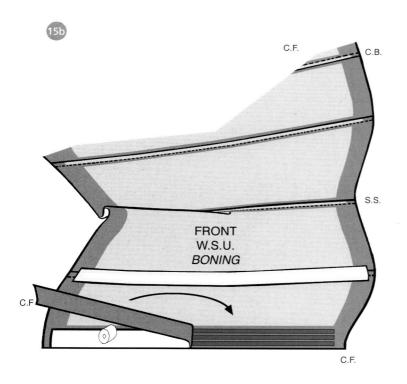

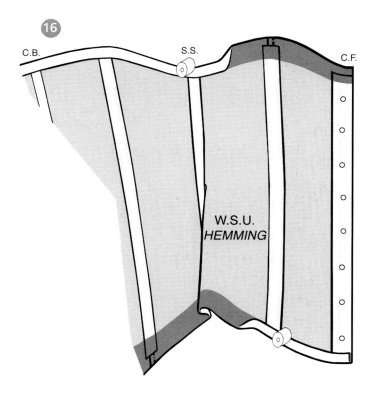

C.B.   S.S.   C.F.

W.S.U.
HEMMING

16 Mark the position of the eyelets
   down the fabric strip or tape and
   fix them in place.

Finishing a latex garment

When you have completed your garment, turn it inside out. Load a large brush with talcum powder or French chalk and dust every seam liberally. Then give the whole inside of the garment a generous covering.

Turn the garment the right side out and inspect it for any extraneous blobs or patches of glue. Sometimes, when the seams are overlapped by less that 8cm ($^5/_{16}$in), unsightly glue is visible.

Next, carry out the following steps to bring the garment to a glorious liquid sheen:

1   Clean any glue away with a cloth soaked in thinner. Allow the thinner to dry.

2   Use a household cleaning sponge and warm water to wash the garment down, removing any excess talc or dust.

3   Dry with an absorbent cloth.

4   Clean the whole outside of the garment with thinner.

5   Apply the PVC dressing or silicone spray.

6   Buff with a soft cloth to a high shine.

Wearing
and storing

To preserve and enjoy wearing a latex garment, be aware of these simple rules:

1   Use clean hands if handling lighter colours, as transference of metal residue from money or jewellery may stain the garment.

2   Remove any watches or sharp jewellery you may be wearing. They can easily catch and pierce the latex, causing it to rip.

3   Give the inside of the garment a dusting of talc so that it does not stick to your skin as you put it on.

4   With a tight garment gently ease it on. Latex is strong but not indestructible. Be aware that the seams are the weak points and although they will withstand lots of stretching, do not tug at them excessively.

5   Give the garment a final polish once it has been put on, as some talc and dust often finds its way to the outside.

6   Store the garment inside out in a cool, dark place, away from direct sunlight. On light-coloured latex, if there are any metal parts such as zips or press studs, make sure these are not in direct contact with any other part of the garment by slipping in a piece plastic or thick paper as a barrier.

Suppliers

Latex

Four D Rubber Co. Ltd
Delves Road
Heanor Gate Industrial Estate
Heanor
Derbyshire
DE75 7SJ

Tel: ++44(0) 1773 763134.
Fax: ++44(0) 1773 763 136
(This company also provides a screen printing service.)

Pentonville Rubber Ltd
104/106 Pentonville Road
London N1 9JB

Tel: ++44(0)0207 837 7553/ 4582
Fax: ++44(0)207 287 7392
Email: queries@pentonvillerubber.co.uk
Website: www.pentonvillerubber.co.uk

The Cloth House
98 Berwick Street
Soho
London W1F 0QJ

Tel/Fax:++44(0)20 7287 1555

Glue and thinner
(Bostik 3851 & Bostik 6009)

The General Engineers' Supply Company (1937) Ltd
555 High Road
Leytonstone
London E11 4PD

Tel: ++44(0)20 8556 0201
Fax: ++44(0)20 8558 9305
Email: gens@engineers555.freeserve.co.uk

Polish

Micro-Chemical Products Ltd (for PVC dressing)
24a Grove Road
London SW13 OHH

Tel: ++44(0)208 876 7775

Moreplan Ltd (for silicone spray)
56 Great Titchfield Street
London W1W 7DF

Tel: ++44(0)207 636 1887
Fax: ++44(0)207 637 9597
Web: www.morplan.com

Skin Two Ltd
Unit 105
Avro House
Havelock Terrace
London SW8 4A5

Tel: ++44(0)207 720 8844
Email: orders@skintwo.com
Web: www.skintwo.com

House Of Harlot Ltd
88-90 Holloway Road
London N7 8GJ

Tel: ++44(0)20 7700 1441
Fax: ++44(0)20 7700 6967
Web: www.house-of-harlot.com

Pleaters

Ciment Pleating Ltd

Unit 20
Bates Road
Harold Wood
Essex
RM3 OHU

Tel:++44(0)1708 340043
Fax:++44(0)1708 349977
Email: pleating@f-ciment.demon.co.uk
Web: www.cimentpleating.co.uk

Pattern cutting books and equipment

R.D.Franks Ltd

Market Place
London W1

Tel:++44(0)207 636 1244
Fax:++44(0)207 436 4904
Email: info@rdfranks.co.uk

Morplan Ltd

See page 103

Acknowledgements

A big thank you to Andrew Woodwood for the photographs. Many thanks are due to the Tun Abdul Kasak Research Centre, Brickendonbury, Hertford, for the use of information contained in their website. I would like to thank Four D Rubber for their help and advice, and also Oshrat Gal.

Index